BIOGRAPHIES *of the* NEW WORLD

LEIF ERIKSSON, HENRY HUDSON, CHARLES DARWIN, AND MORE

IMPACT ON AMERICA: COLLECTIVE BIOGRAPHIES

BIOGRAPHIES of the NEW WORLD

LEIF ERIKSSON, HENRY HUDSON, CHARLES DARWIN, AND MORE

Edited by Michael Anderson

Britannica
Educational Publishing
IN ASSOCIATION WITH

SKOKIE PUBLIC LIBRARY

Published in 2013 by Britannica Educational Publishing
(a trademark of Encyclopædia Britannica, Inc.)
in association with Rosen Educational Services, LLC
29 East 21st Street, New York, NY 10010.

Copyright © 2013 Encyclopædia Britannica, Inc. Britannica, Encyclopædia Britannica, and the Thistle logo are registered trademarks of Encyclopædia Britannica, Inc. All rights reserved.

Rosen Educational Services materials copyright © 2013 Rosen Educational Services, LLC.
All rights reserved.

Distributed exclusively by Rosen Educational Services.
For a listing of additional Britannica Educational Publishing titles, call toll free (800) 237-9932.

First Edition

Britannica Educational Publishing
J.E. Luebering: Director, Core Reference Group, Encyclopædia Britannica
Adam Augustyn: Assistant Manager, Encyclopædia Britannica

Anthony L. Green: Editor, Compton's by Britannica
Michael Anderson: Senior Editor, Compton's by Britannica
Andrea R. Field: Senior Editor, Compton's by Britannica
Sherman Hollar: Associate Editor, Compton's by Britannica

Marilyn L. Barton: Senior Coordinator, Production Control
Steven Bosco: Director, Editorial Technologies
Lisa S. Braucher: Senior Producer and Data Editor
Yvette Charboneau: Senior Copy Editor
Kathy Nakamura: Manager, Media Acquisition

Rosen Educational Services
Nicholas Croce: Editor
Nelson Sá: Art Director
Cindy Reiman: Photography Manager
Karen Huang: Photo Researcher
Brian Garvey: Designer, Cover Design
Introduction by Nicholas Croce

Library of Congress Cataloging-in-Publication Data

Biographies of the New World: Leif Eriksson, Henry Hudson, Charles Darwin, and more/edited by Michael Anderson.—1st ed.
　　p. cm.—(Impact on America: collective biographies)
"In association with Britannica Educational Publishing, Rosen Educational Services."
Includes bibliographical references and index.
ISBN 978-1-61530-672-5 (library binding)
1. Explorers—America—Biography—Juvenile literature. 2. America—Discovery and exploration—Juvenile literature. 3. Explorers—America—History—Juvenile literature.
I. Anderson, Michael, 1972–
E101.B58 2011
910.92'2—dc23
[B]

2011043717

Manufactured in the United States of America

Cover, p. 3 © www.istockphoto.com/ Iakov Kalinin (beach with shell), © www.istockphoto.com/subjug (parchment paper), © www.istockphoto.com/spxChrome (locket), Hulton Archive/Getty Images (Leif Eriksson, H.M.S. Beagle), Library of Congress Prints and Photographs Division (Charles Darwin); back cover © www.istockphoto.com/Sodafish bvba; interior background images © www.istockphoto.com/oliopi (geometric), © www.istockphoto.com/Bill Noll (floral)

CONTENTS

Introduction 8

Ch. 1 Leif Eriksson 12
Ch. 2 Christopher Columbus 16
Ch. 3 John Cabot 24
Ch. 4 Pedro Álvares Cabral 27
Ch. 5 Amerigo Vespucci 29
Ch. 6 Juan Ponce de León 32
Ch. 7 Vasco Núñez de Balboa 33
Ch. 8 Ferdinand Magellan 36
Ch. 9 Giovanni da Verrazzano 43
Ch. 10 Hernán Cortés 45
Ch. 11 Francisco Pizarro 50
Ch. 12 Pánfilo de Narváez 55
Ch. 13 Hernando de Soto 57
Ch. 14 Francisco Vázquez
         de Coronado 60
Ch. 15 Jacques Cartier 63
Ch. 16 Sir Francis Drake 65
Ch. 17 Sir Walter Raleigh 70

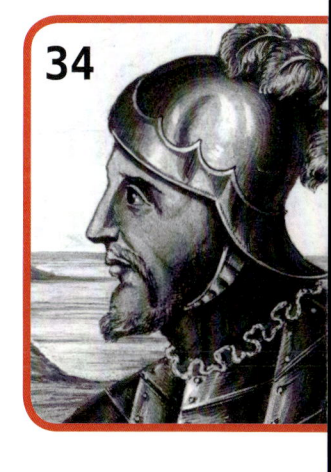

CONTENTS

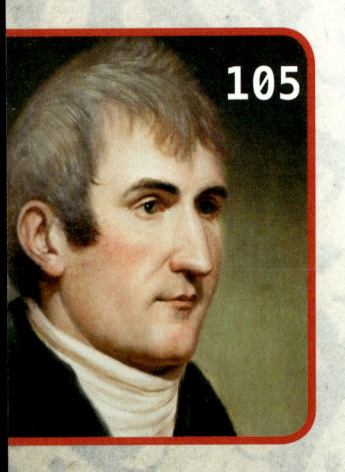

Ch. 18 Samuel de Champlain 76
Ch. 19 Henry Hudson 80
Ch. 20 Jacques Marquette 83
Ch. 21 Louis Jolliet 88
Ch. 22 Sieur de La Salle 90
Ch. 23 James Cook 97
Ch. 24 David Thompson 101
Ch. 25 Meriwether Lewis 104
Ch. 26 William Clark 112
Ch. 27 Alexander von Humboldt . . 114
Ch. 28 Charles Darwin 118

Conclusion 122
Glossary 124
For More Information 127
Bibliography 131
Index 132

INTRODUCTION

The New World refers to the Western Hemisphere, namely what is now North and South America. At the time the name originated, these regions were first being explored by European navigators such as Christopher Columbus, John Cabot, and Amerigo Vespucci. Peter Martyr d'Anghiera, an Italian scholar of the era, used the term New World in his chronicles of Columbus's voyages and other early Spanish explorations. Vespucci and Giovanni da Verrazzano also used the term when referring to their voyages across the Atlantic.

These early explorations of the New World, beginning with Columbus's voyage of 1492, came during a great period of exploration known as the Age of Discovery. It was a time of great economic expansion for Europe, which, along with Asia and Africa, came to be known as the Old World. In the 15th and 16th centuries, explorers from Spain, Portugal, France, England, and the Netherlands, among other powers, charted these territories, largely in search of new trade routes. In addition to Columbus and Vespucci, some of the most notable names of this era included Juan Ponce de León, Ferdinand Magellan, Hernán

Cortés, and Hernando de Soto. Though they were all in search of something in their explorations, the New World offered different opportunities to each of them. While many sought new lands and trade routes for their countries, others had more personal motives, such as wealth and fame. Cortés, de Soto, and others followed reports of civilizations rich in gold, for instance. Ponce de León sought the fabled Fountain of Youth.

In the course of their expeditions, many New World explorers mapped the regions they covered and documented their findings, giving those back home a picture of these newly found lands and the notion that the world was far more vast than they had ever imagined. In the late 18th century James Cook, an explorer and skilled mapmaker, surveyed much of the Pacific, including the coastline of northwestern North America. Between 1804 and 1806 Meriwether Lewis and William Clark charted the newly purchased Louisiana Territory for the United States. In addition to mapping the land, Lewis and Clark documented the native peoples and described 178 plants and 122 animals previously unknown to science. Around the same time, Alexander von Humboldt traveled extensively in Central and South America, returning home with valuable information on the weather, geology, and plants and animals of those regions. Another scientist whose work was inspired by a New World expedition was Charles Darwin. His observations of the natural world during his voyage around South America in the 1830s were pivotal to his formulation of the theory of evolution.

Before the 15th century the New World was a place of great unknowns. The explorers profiled in this book, though motivated by different goals, all played a role in filling those gaps in knowledge. They opened the eyes of the Old World to new lands, peoples, cultures, and plants and animals—and a better understanding of the world in general.

CHAPTER 1

LEIF ERIKSSON

The first European to land on the North American continent was a Viking seaman named Leif Eriksson (or Ericson). He was the second son of the explorer Erik the Red, who was originally from Norway but later settled in Iceland, where Leif was born. In about AD 982 Erik took his family on an expedition to an unknown land—Greenland. Leif grew up in Brattahild (now Qassiarsuk), on Greenland's southwest coast.

Different accounts of Leif's voyages appear in two Icelandic sagas, histories about kings and other heroes associated with Iceland. According to the *Saga of Erik*, in 1000 Leif voyaged to Norway, where he spent a winter at the court of Norway's Christian king, Olaf I Tryggvason. When Leif returned home, he converted his mother to Christianity. She built the first Christian church in Greenland; its foundations and those of other Viking buildings may be seen in Qassiarsuk.

According to the *Saga of Erik*, Leif's ship was blown off course on his return from Norway and was carried westward to North

An engraved portrait of Leif Eriksson. Hulton Archive/Getty Images

America. The *Saga of the Greenlanders*, which many modern scholars believe to be more reliable, offers a different account. It tells that Leif learned of a land far to the west from an Icelander named Bjarni Herjulfsson, who had sighted it but had not gone ashore. In about 1000 Leif gathered a crew of about 35 and set off from Greenland for the unknown land. They put ashore at a place described as a barren tableland of flat rocks backed by great ice mountains.

Going to sea again, they traveled southward, dropping anchor off a level, wooded land with broad stretches of white sand. They called it Markland (Wood Land). Once again they sailed to the south. This time they went ashore where the land was green with "fields of self-sown wheat," trees, and sweet wild grapes. They named it Vinland (Wine Land) and built shelters and spent the winter there. After exploring the area, they returned home to Greenland. Leif earned his nickname Leif the Lucky on this trip, when he rescued a shipwrecked party of 15.

It is not known for certain where in North America Leif's expedition landed, but it was probably somewhere along the Atlantic coastline of what is now eastern or northeastern Canada. He may have landed on the coast of Newfoundland. In 1963 archaeologists uncovered the remains of a Viking settlement at L'Anse aux Meadows, at the northernmost tip of the island. Radiocarbon dating of charcoal found in hearths shows that the site was used in about AD 1000.

In about 1003 Leif's brother Thorvald led an expedition to Vinland. Thorfinn Karlsefni, an Icelander, later established a colony of about 130 people in Vinland. His son Snorri was the first child of European descent born in North America. After living in Vinland for three years, however, the settlers abandoned their colony because of conflicts with local Indians (First Nations). In about 1013 Leif's half-sister Freydis led an unsuccessful expedition to Vinland; it was the last known Viking attempt at colonizing North America.

CHAPTER 2

CHRISTOPHER COLUMBUS

On the morning of Oct. 12, 1492, Christopher Columbus stepped ashore on an island in what has since become known as the Americas. The arrival of his ships in the Western Hemisphere was one of the pivotal events in world history. It opened up a new world for Europeans and initiated the spread of Western civilization to a new hemisphere. Though the Vikings had visited North America five centuries earlier, Columbus's voyages had many more lasting effects. They began an unstoppable wave of exploration and settlement that would transform the Americas.

Columbus is a controversial figure. For many years he was honored as the "discoverer" of the Americas. More recently, however, scholars have focused on the devastating effects of the European conquest on the Native Americans. The slave trade and diseases carried by the Europeans had a disastrous impact on native cultures. This reassessment has greatly diminished the sense of heroism in Columbus's legacy. It does not, however, detract from his towering

An illustration, circa 1475, of Italian explorer Christopher Columbus.
Stock Montage/Archive Photos/Getty Images

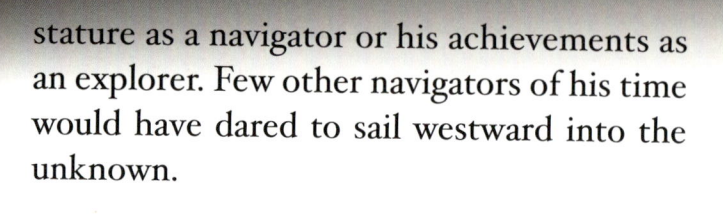

stature as a navigator or his achievements as an explorer. Few other navigators of his time would have dared to sail westward into the unknown.

Early Life and Career

Cristoforo Colombo was born in 1451, probably in Genoa, Italy. (English-speaking peoples later changed the Italian form of his name to Christopher Columbus.) He was the son of a wool weaver and had little or no schooling.

Columbus worked for his father until he was 22. He probably went out with the sardine fishing fleets, as other Genoese boys did, and he may have sailed along the coast or over to Corsica on business for his father. He made at least one trip to the North African coast. On these longer voyages he learned the elements of seamanship.

After surviving a shipwreck off the coast of Portugal in 1476, Columbus settled in Lisbon. At this time Portugal was the world's greatest seafaring nation. Many Genoese had prospered in Lisbon, and Columbus saw his chance to become a sea captain under the Portuguese flag.

To earn his living he became a chart maker, and he also made several trading voyages. In 1479 he married Felipa Perestrello, with whom he had one son, Diego.

In the 1480s Columbus started planning a voyage to discover a sea route to Asia. Europeans were eager for Asian goods, but these goods were scarce and expensive because they had to come by a perilous overland route. Ships could carry them more cheaply and in greater quantity. To reach India, China, Japan, and the East Indies, the Portuguese were already probing for an eastern sea route around Africa. Another possibility was a western sea route across the Atlantic and beyond.

In 1484 Columbus applied for ships and men from King John II of Portugal. The application was refused. Meanwhile, Columbus's wife had died. Taking his son, he journeyed to Spain to seek support from King Ferdinand and Queen Isabella. While awaiting a decision, Columbus took Beatriz Enríquez de Harana as his common-law wife. They later had one son, Ferdinand.

Finally, in January 1492, the Spanish sovereigns agreed to finance the expedition. They provided three ships: the *Niña*, the *Pinta*, and the *Santa María*. Columbus commanded the *Santa María* himself and selected captains to lead the other ships.

THE FIRST VOYAGE

At dawn on August 3, 1492, the three ships hoisted anchor and left the Spanish harbor town of Palos. First they reached the Canary Islands, off the northwest African mainland. After nearly a month in the Canaries, the ships left the islands on September 6 and headed west.

For the most part the passage was smooth and the winds were steady. As the days passed, however, the crew could not see how they could sail home against winds that had blown them steadily west. By early October the crew was ready to rebel. Columbus had to agree to turn back if land was not sighted within three days.

On October 12 a sailor aboard the *Pinta* made the first sighting of the New World. The little fleet had reached the Bahama Islands in the Caribbean Sea. Columbus named the first land sighted San Salvador (probably now Watling Island). The native inhabitants called the island Guanahani. Columbus, believing San Salvador to be an island of the East Indies in Asia, called the native people Indians. Columbus took possession of the island in the name of the rulers of Spain.

Sailing on, Columbus stopped at islands he named Santa María de la Concepción (now Rum Cay), Fernandina (Long Island), and Isabela (Crooked Island). He then sailed south to the north coast of Cuba. He named this island Juana. On December 6, 1492, Columbus reached the north coast of Hispaniola. Here he found some gold to bring back to Spain. Early Christmas morning the *Santa María* went aground. Its bottom was so badly torn that the ship had to be abandoned. From its timber Columbus built a small fort, La Navidad. Columbus left 39 men to guard the fort.

On January 16, 1493, the *Niña* and the *Pinta* began the return voyage. They carried gold, parrots and other strange animals and plants, some Indian cloth and ornaments, and several Indians. A stormy eastward passage separated the two ships and did much damage. Columbus, on the *Niña*, landed at Lisbon for repairs. The *Pinta* made port at the Spanish town of Bayona, to the north of Portugal. In

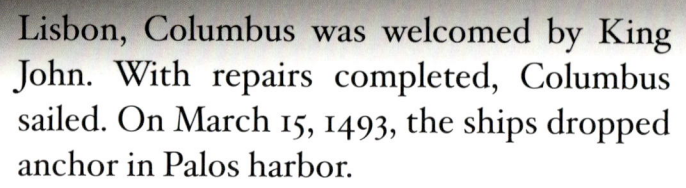

Lisbon, Columbus was welcomed by King John. With repairs completed, Columbus sailed. On March 15, 1493, the ships dropped anchor in Palos harbor.

The court was at Barcelona, and the Spanish king and queen welcomed Columbus there. To the court Columbus took six of the Indians, the gold, and some of the plants and animals. The sovereigns rose to greet Columbus and seated him at their right. All honors and titles promised him were confirmed. This was the height of Columbus's glory.

LATER VOYAGES

Columbus made three more trips to the New World: 1493 to 1496, 1498 to 1500, and 1502 to 1504. On the first return voyage he had 17 ships and about 1,200 men. At Hispaniola, Columbus found that La Navidad had been burned and the 39 sailors slain. A new colony was started. Columbus explored the coasts of Jamaica, Cuba, and Hispaniola.

On the next voyage he first sighted Trinidad. He also explored some of the northeastern shore of South America and the Leeward Islands. Meanwhile, dissatisfied colonists had returned to Spain and complained at court. A new governor was sent to replace Columbus. He arrested Columbus and shipped him back in chains. The monarchs released him and restored his titles. On the final voyage Columbus tried vainly to find a passage to India. He explored the east coast of Central America but lost two ships. The two remaining ships, in poor condition, ran aground on Jamaica in June 1503. Messengers sent by canoe to Hispaniola finally brought rescue ships in June 1504.

Columbus returned to Spain broken in health and spirit. He was not received at court. The king refused to restore his privileges and honors. He was, however, far from poor. He had brought back gold, and he shared in the gold mined in Hispaniola. He died in Valladolid, Spain, on May 20, 1506.

CHAPTER 3

JOHN CABOT

An Italian explorer sailing for England, John Cabot was the first European to reach the shores of North America after the Vikings. England later claimed all of North America on the ground that Cabot was the first explorer to reach the mainland.

The details of Cabot's life and voyages are a subject of debate among historians. It is believed that he was born Giovanni Caboto in Genoa, Italy, in about 1450. As a child he moved with his family to Venice, and he became a citizen of that city in 1476. During the 1470s he developed into a skilled navigator in travels to the eastern Mediterranean for a Venetian mercantile firm involved in the spice trade. Upon learning that the spices originated in the Far East, he came up with a plan for reaching Asia by sailing westward.

By the end of 1495 Cabot had moved to England. There, in the port city of Bristol, he won support for his plan among merchants who hoped for a direct link to the Asian markets. In 1496 Henry VII, the English king, authorized the trip even though he had earlier rejected a similar proposal by Christopher Columbus.

John Cabot and his crew arrive at the coast of North America in 1497. Stock Montage/Archive Photos/Getty Images

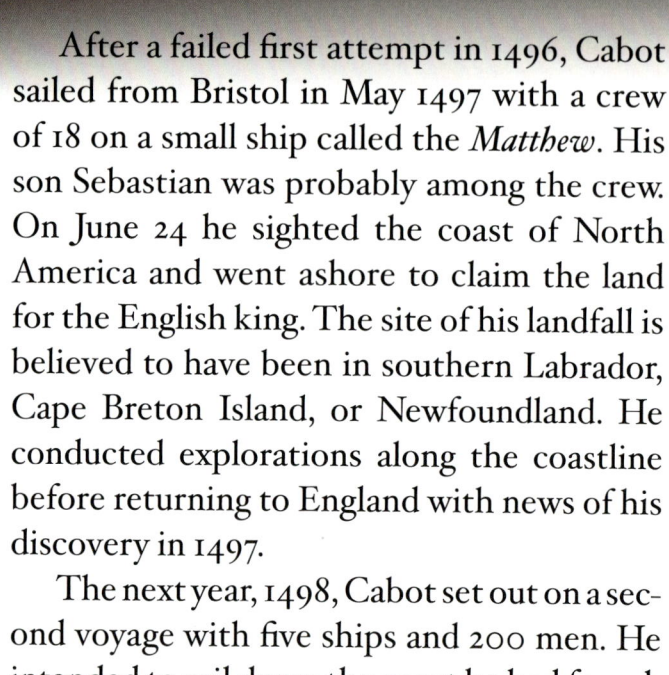

After a failed first attempt in 1496, Cabot sailed from Bristol in May 1497 with a crew of 18 on a small ship called the *Matthew*. His son Sebastian was probably among the crew. On June 24 he sighted the coast of North America and went ashore to claim the land for the English king. The site of his landfall is believed to have been in southern Labrador, Cape Breton Island, or Newfoundland. He conducted explorations along the coastline before returning to England with news of his discovery in 1497.

The next year, 1498, Cabot set out on a second voyage with five ships and 200 men. He intended to sail down the coast he had found, which he believed to be the coast of China. He thus hoped to find Japan. Cabot did not return from this voyage. Some evidence suggests that he reached North America again, but he was probably lost at sea.

CHAPTER 4

PEDRO ÁLVARES CABRAL

The Portuguese navigator Pedro Álvares Cabral is generally credited with the European discovery of Brazil. This vast expanse of land became a port of call on the long voyage from Europe to India and was a major addition to Portugal's large overseas empire.

Pedro Álvares Cabral was born in Belmonte, Portugal, in 1467 or 1468. The son of a noble family with a long tradition of service to the crown, he was educated at the royal court. In 1497 King Manuel I appointed him to the King's Council.

Three years later the king named him commander of the second major Portuguese expedition to India. He was to follow the route taken earlier by Vasco da Gama. Thirteen ships set out from Lisbon on March 9, 1500. Sailing southwestward, they sighted the Brazilian coast on April 22. Cabral landed and met some of the American Indians who lived in the area. Claiming the territory for Portugal, he sent one ship back to inform the king of the discovery.

After only 10 days Cabral sailed on for India. Rounding the Cape of Good Hope, four ships were lost with all hands aboard. The remaining ships arrived at Calicut (now Kozhikode), India, on September 13. Disputes arose with Arab traders, and many Portuguese were killed. In retaliation, Cabral bombarded the city, captured 10 Arab ships, and executed their crews. He then sailed southward to other Indian ports and traded for spices and other goods. Cabral arrived home in Portugal on June 23, 1501, with only four of his original 13 ships.

Although the king was pleased and considered making Cabral head of the next Portuguese expedition, he appointed Vasco da Gama instead. Cabral retired to his estate. He died in about 1520 in Santarém, Portugal.

CHAPTER 5

AMERIGO VESPUCCI

The Americas are named after the merchant, navigator, and explorer Amerigo Vespucci. In a pamphlet printed in 1507, a German cartographer named Martin Waldseemüller suggested that the newly discovered land be named "from Amerigo the discoverer…as if it were the land of Americus or America." Waldseemüller created a large map on which the name America appears for the first time, though it is applied only to South America. The extension of the name to North America came later. Waldseemüller's suggestion resulted in one of the oddities of history—the naming of the Americas after a comparatively unknown man who sailed on early expeditions to South America and wrote about them, instead of after Christopher Columbus, the European "discoverer" of the Americas. Nevertheless, as a result of his voyages, Vespucci and scholars first realized that the Americas were indeed a "New World" and not part of Asia, as Columbus and others had thought.

Amerigo Vespucci (or Americus Vespucius, as the name is spelled in Latin)

Amerigo Vespucci is greeted by mythical gods and creatures, including Neptune and mermaids, upon arriving in the New World. **Three Lions/Hulton Archive/Getty Images**

was born in Florence, Italy, probably in 1454. He entered the Medici family's banking and commercial business and in 1491 was sent to Seville, Spain. There he helped to fit out ships for Columbus's second and third voyages. By 1496 he was manager of the Seville agency.

In a letter written in 1504, Vespucci claimed to have made four voyages to the Americas. Modern historians are not sure, however, whether he really sailed on two or four voyages. According to Vespucci, he made his first voyage in 1497–98 to the southeast coast of North America. Most scholars reject his version of this voyage. Vespucci did, however, serve as navigator on a Spanish expedition to South America under Alonzo de Ojeda in 1499–1500. On this voyage, Vespucci is believed to have "discovered" the mouth of the Amazon River. He next commanded a Portuguese expedition in 1501–02 to the coast of Brazil. Vespucci might have sighted Guanabara Bay (Rio de Janeiro's bay) and sailed to the Río de la Plata, making him the first European to discover that estuary. It is uncertain whether he sailed again for Portugal in 1503–04. Although Vespucci later helped to prepare other expeditions, he never again joined one in person. He held the influential post of master navigator in Seville from 1508 until his death there in 1512.

CHAPTER 6

JUAN PONCE DE LEÓN

A Spanish soldier and explorer, Juan Ponce de León is probably best remembered for his search for the fabled Fountain of Youth. He was born in the province of León in northwestern Spain in 1460. In 1493 he accompanied Christopher Columbus on his second voyage to America. Ponce de León established a colony on Puerto Rico in 1508 and was made governor in 1509. In Puerto Rico he heard a legend about an island called Bimini, where there was said to be a spring that restored youth to all who bathed in it. It is said he was seeking this spring when he discovered Florida.

He sailed from Puerto Rico in March 1513. On Easter Sunday he sighted the coast. A few days later he landed on Florida's east coast, near what is now St. Augustine. He named the place La Florida after the Spanish term for Easter Sunday—*Pascua florida*, or "flowery feast." He then sailed around the peninsula and up the west coast. He returned to Florida in 1521. Wounded during an Indian attack, he was taken back to Cuba, where he soon died. Ponce de León is buried in the cathedral at San Juan, Puerto Rico.

CHAPTER 7

VASCO NÚÑEZ DE BALBOA

The first European to look upon the Pacific Ocean from the shores of the New World was Vasco Núñez de Balboa. The Spanish adventurer and explorer also led a colony in what is now Panama that was the first stable European settlement on the mainland of the Americas.

Balboa was born in 1475 in Jerez de los Caballeros, Spain, into the lower ranks of the nobility. In 1500 he sailed for the Americas on an exploring expedition to what is now Colombia. He later settled on the Caribbean island of Hispaniola. There his unsuccessful attempts at farming led him into debt. In 1510, hoping to escape his creditors, he stowed away on a ship bound for the new colony of San Sebastián, on the northern coast of Colombia.

When the ship arrived at San Sebastián, the expedition discovered that the colony's founder had fled and abandoned the survivors. Balboa persuaded his superiors to transfer the colony to Darién, on the Isthmus of Panama, where the colonists founded the town of Santa María de la Antigua. Balboa soon became the head of the colony.

LEIF ERIKSSON, HENRY HUDSON, CHARLES DARWIN, AND MORE

Vasco Núñez de Balboa, circa 1510. Hulton Archive/Getty Images

From local Indians, Balboa learned of a great ocean beyond the mountains and of the gold to be found there. He sent word to Spain that he needed reinforcements to explore the area. In Spain an expedition was organized, but Balboa was not given command. The king instead sent Pedro Arias Dávila as commander and as governor of Darién.

Meanwhile Balboa, without waiting for reinforcements, had set out across the isthmus. It took about 25 days for his party of 190 Spaniards and hundreds of Indians to cross 45 miles (70 kilometers) of dense jungle. On September 29, 1513, Balboa reached the shores of the Pacific Ocean, which he called the South Sea. He took possession of the ocean and all lands washed by it in the name of the Spanish monarch.

When Balboa returned to Darién, conflict arose immediately between him and the new governor. Balboa received grudging permission to explore the South Sea but was then summoned home and arrested on the false charge of instigating a rebellion. He was found guilty and was beheaded on Jan. 12, 1519, in Acla, near Darién.

CHAPTER 8

FERDINAND MAGELLAN

The first European to sail across the Pacific Ocean was the Portuguese navigator and explorer Ferdinand Magellan. He was the first person to discover a route by which ships could sail a complete circle around the world. The Strait of Magellan is named for him. This strait, located at the southern tip of South America, proved to be the long-sought connection between the Atlantic and Pacific oceans. Sailing for the Spanish king Charles I (later Holy Roman Emperor Charles V), Magellan proved in his explorations that Earth is round. He also established a new route from Europe to the riches of the East, a route that involved sailing to the west.

Fernão de Magalhães was born around 1480, probably in Sabrosa or Porto, Portugal. (Ferdinand Magellan is the English spelling of his name.) The son of Portuguese nobles, he began his career by serving with distinction in naval campaigns in the East Indies and Morocco. After several years, he twice requested a small increase in his pay. The Portuguese

FERDINAND MAGELLAN

A statue of Ferdinand Magellan stands in a park in Punta Arenas, Chile.
Bruce Dale/National Geographic Image Collection/Getty Images

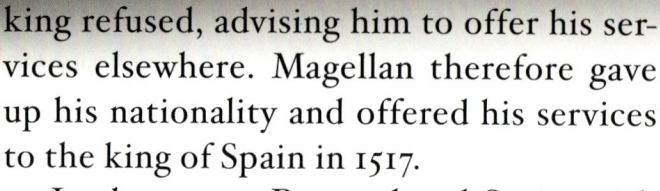

king refused, advising him to offer his services elsewhere. Magellan therefore gave up his nationality and offered his services to the king of Spain in 1517.

In the 1490s, Portugal and Spain, with approval from the pope, had divided rights of exploration in the New World between themselves. The Portuguese claimed that all the islands of the East Indies lay in their territory. Magellan claimed that many of them, including the rich Spice Islands (or Moluccas, now in Indonesia), actually lay in Spain's territory. He said that the Portuguese maps had been falsified to conceal this fact. Magellan offered to use his knowledge of Portuguese secrets to prove his claim. He planned to reach the Spice Islands by sailing westward through a strait that he hoped to discover at the southern tip of America. The Spanish king finally accepted Magellan's proposal.

On September 20, 1519, Magellan set sail from Sanlúcar de Barrameda, in southwestern Spain, in command of five small vessels. He sailed across the Atlantic Ocean and down the coast of South America until cold weather and winter storms forced him to seek winter quarters. He had to put down a mutiny by force, and one of his ships was wrecked while surveying the area.

Sailing again in August 1520, Magellan's fleet eventually rounded a promontory. On October 21 he sighted what he guessed to be the sought-for strait. Two ships went ahead and reported that the strait led to an ocean beyond. The fleet proceeded. What they had thought to be the ocean, however, proved to be only a large bay in the strait. At a council with his navigators Magellan decided to go on.

For more than a month Magellan battled his way through the stormy 325-mile (525-kilometer) passage that now bears his name. One vessel deserted, sailing back to Spain. Nevertheless, Magellan insisted that the remaining three ships continue on. On November 28 he reached the ocean that Vasco Núñez de Balboa had "discovered" seven years before. Because the ocean then looked so calm, Magellan named it the Pacific, which means "peaceable."

At first the voyage on the Pacific went well. After a month of sailing, however, terrible hardships struck the fleet. The food and water ran low, and the sailors were reduced to eating the leather fittings of the ship. Many of the crew died of scurvy. The fleet sailed about 100 days before arriving at the islands that are now called the Philippines.

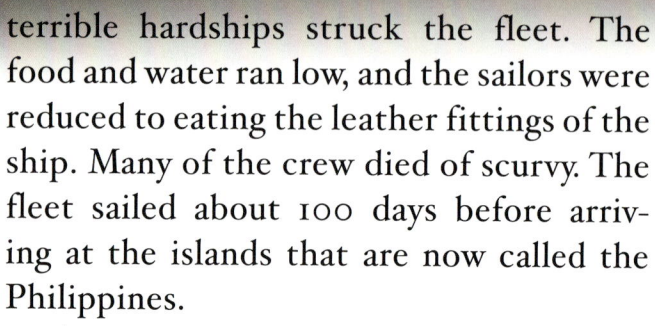

At Limasawa, Magellan negotiated Spain's first alliance in the Pacific. At Cebu he converted the king and his chief followers to Christianity. Magellan sailed from Cebu to the neighboring island of Mactan. There he and his men became involved in a fight with islanders, and Magellan was killed on April 27, 1521.

Under the leadership of Juan Sebastián del Cano, the sailors burned one of the three remaining vessels and sailed to the Spice Islands. Another ship started to leak and had to be abandoned. The last remaining vessel, the *Victoria*, commanded by Cano, set out for home. Leaky but laden with valuable spices, the *Victoria* rounded the Cape of Good Hope at Africa's southern tip. It dropped anchor in the harbor of Seville on September 9, 1522. After a voyage of slightly more than three years, it had circled the globe.

Contrary to popular belief, Magellan succeeded in sailing around the world before his death. He did not encompass the globe on a single voyage, however. On a previous eastbound voyage to the East Indies, he had gone beyond the longitude (east-west position) of the Philippines. Thus, at the time he was killed, he had already overlapped his earlier course.

Mercator projection map of the route taken by Ferdinand Magellan during the first circumnavigation of the globe.
Universal Images Group/Hulton Archive/Getty Images

In the history of discovery no name ranks higher than that of Magellan. He opened the Pacific Ocean to new exploration and trade. John Fiske, a 19th-century American historian, said: "The voyage thus ended was doubtless the greatest feat of navigation that has ever been performed, and nothing can be imagined that would surpass it except a journey to some other planet."

CHAPTER 9

GIOVANNI DA VERRAZZANO

Sailing for France, the Italian navigator and explorer Giovanni da Verrazzano was the first European to sight New York and Narragansett bays. His explorations gave France its claim to the New World.

Verrazzano was born in 1485 in Tuscany (now in Italy). After his education in Florence, he moved to Dieppe, France, and entered that country's maritime service. He made several voyages to the Levant (the land at the eastern end of the Mediterranean Sea), and in 1523 he secured two ships for a voyage backed by the French king to discover a westward passage to Asia. In January 1524 he sailed one of those vessels, *La Dauphine*, to the New World and reached Cape Fear about the beginning of March. Verrazzano then sailed northward, exploring the eastern coast of North America. He made several discoveries on the voyage, including the sites of present-day New York Harbor, Block Island, and Narragansett Bay. He was the first European explorer to name newly discovered North American sites after persons and places in the Old World.

Verrazzano wrote interesting, though sometimes inaccurate, accounts of the lands and people that he encountered. His explorations ended at the eastern part of Newfoundland. He returned to France on July 8, 1524.

Verrazzano undertook two more voyages to the Americas. In 1527 he commanded a fleet of ships on an expedition to Brazil that returned profitable dyewood to France. His final voyage began in the spring of 1528, when he sailed with his brother, Girolamo, from Dieppe with two or three ships. The fleet sailed to Florida, the Bahamas, and finally the Lesser Antilles. He anchored there off one of the islands (apparently Guadeloupe), went ashore, and was captured, killed, and eaten by cannibals.

CHAPTER 10

HERNÁN CORTÉS

The Spanish conquistador, or conqueror, Hernán Cortés overthrew the Aztec Empire of Mexico in 1521. He thus captured the great wealth of the Aztec for Spain, and Mexico remained under Spanish rule for three centuries.

Hernán Cortés (or Hernando Cortez) was born in 1485 in the small town of Medellín in southwestern Spain. When he was 19, he sailed for the island of Hispaniola, then the Spanish headquarters in the West Indies. He worked as a farmer and public official before he sailed under Diego Velásquez to help conquer Cuba in 1511. Velásquez became the governor, and Cortés was elected *alcalde* (mayor-judge) of the town of Santiago.

In 1518 Juan de Grijalba returned from an exploring expedition to Mexico with reports of a civilization rich in gold. Velásquez picked Cortés to establish a colony there. Velásquez soon suspected Cortés of ambitions beyond his orders and canceled the expedition. Cortés, however, defied Velásquez. He assembled about 500 soldiers and set sail on February 18, 1519, with 11 ships. After rounding the Yucatán peninsula, they touched Mexico on the coast of what is now the state of Tabasco. Local Indians gave the Spaniards a peace offering of presents, including many slave women. One of them became Cortés's interpreter, adviser, and lover. He gave her the Spanish name Marina.

Cortés continued up the Mexican coast and founded the town of Veracruz. There, to prevent all thought of retreat, he destroyed his ships. Leaving a small force on the coast, Cortés led the remainder into the interior. The Tlaxcalans attacked—300 Indians to every Spaniard. After three battles, these Indians became allies of the Spaniards. Cortés formed alliances with many tribes who hated their Aztec overlords. These alliances were important to the Spaniards' ultimate success.

On Nov. 8, 1519, Cortés reached Tenochtitlán (now Mexico City), which was the Aztec capital. He was graciously received there by Montezuma II, the Aztec emperor. Cortés soon captured Montezuma.

Hernán Cortés. © Photos.com/Jupiterimages

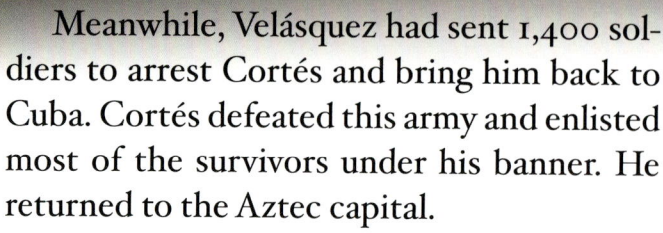

Meanwhile, Velásquez had sent 1,400 soldiers to arrest Cortés and bring him back to Cuba. Cortés defeated this army and enlisted most of the survivors under his banner. He returned to the Aztec capital.

The leader of the Spanish garrison in Tenochtitlán had slaughtered 600 Mexican nobles. As Cortés and his men reached the heart of the city in mid-1520, they were attacked by thousands of Aztec warriors. The Spaniards fought their way out of the capital, eventually making their way back to their Tlaxcalan allies.

Cortés besieged Tenochtitlán again in the spring of 1521. This time the siege included the use of ships with cannon. The Spanish conquest was also made easier by diseases such as smallpox and measles that were decimating the Aztec. The Spaniards and their Indian allies fought their way through the city, finally capturing it on August 13, 1521. This was the end of the great empire of the Aztec.

Cortés became ruler of the enormous territory he had conquered, but his career was damaged by the political attacks of Spanish rivals. After a disastrous expedition in 1524 to the Honduran jungles, he was forced to retire. In 1528 he returned to Spain, where he was received with great honor by King Charles V. Cortés was made marqués (marquis) del Valle. However, he had no skill for court politics. When he returned to Mexico, he went merely as a military commander. He explored Lower California from 1534 to 1535 and served against the pirates of Algiers in 1541. He died near Seville, Spain, on December 2, 1547.

CHAPTER 11

FRANCISCO PIZARRO

The conquest of Peru by an obscure adventurer is one of the most dramatic episodes in the history of the New World. Until he was nearly 50 years old, Francisco Pizarro, serving as a minor Spanish official on the Isthmus of Panama, had nothing to show for years of toil and peril but a small holding of land. Little more than a decade later, he had conquered the fabulously wealthy empire of the Incas and had bestowed on Spain the richest of its American possessions. He also founded the city of Lima, now the capital of Peru.

Pizarro was born in about 1475 in Trujillo, a small town near Cáceres, Spain. The illegitimate son of a Spanish captain, he spent his childhood with his grandparents in one of Spain's poorest regions. He apparently never learned to read or write.

Pizarro traveled to the Caribbean island of Hispaniola in 1502 with the governor of that Spanish colony. He took part in an expedition to Colombia in 1510, and three years later, he accompanied Vasco Nuñez de Balboa on a journey that ended in the discovery of the Pacific Ocean. From 1519 to 1523 he served as mayor of the town of Panama.

In 1523, hearing of a vast and wealthy Indian empire to the south, Pizarro enlisted the help of two friends to form an expedition to explore and conquer the land. A soldier named Diego de Almagro provided the equipment, and the vicar of Panama, Hernando de Luque, furnished the funds.

A first expedition resulted in disaster after two years of suffering and hardship. When a second expedition in 1526 fared little better, Pizarro sent Almagro back to Panama for reinforcements. He and part of the group remained on an island.

Instead of sending help, the governor of Panama sent vessels to bring back the expedition. Pizarro refused to return. Drawing a line on the sand, he asked all who wanted a share in his enterprise to join him. Thirteen men crossed the line. Pizarro's friends persuaded the governor to send one vessel. Pizarro used it to explore the coast of Peru. He then sailed to Spain to ask authority to conquer Peru. This was granted. He left Spain on January 19, 1530, and sailed from Panama the following year. He had three vessels, which contained fewer than 200 men and about 40 horses.

BIOGRAPHIES OF THE NEW WORLD:
LEIF ERIKSSON, HENRY HUDSON, CHARLES DARWIN, AND MORE

Undated engraving of Francisco Pizarro. Library of Congress, Washington, D.C.

Thus, after seven years of hardship and disappointment, the adventurers started the conquest of Peru. Pizarro spent a year conquering the coastal settlements. Then he marched inland to the city of Cajamarca. There he met with emissaries of Atahuallpa, the Inca emperor. Atahuallpa accepted an invitation to visit the Spanish commander and arrived attended by crowds of unarmed Incas. Pizarro's followers were armed and waiting. Atahuallpa was to regret trusting Pizarro. When he refused to convert to Christianity or to accept the Spanish king as his sovereign, Pizarro and his men seized the Inca emperor, and the Spaniards slaughtered 2,000 Indians.

Atahuallpa offered as ransom to fill with gold a room 17 by 22 feet (5 by 7 meters) to a point as high as a man could reach and to fill it twice over with silver. Pizarro accepted the ransom. Soon afterward, however, he had Atahuallpa executed. Pizarro then marched to Cuzco and set up Manco, Atahuallpa's brother, as nominal sovereign. In 1535 he founded Ciudad de los Reyes (City of the Kings), which is now Lima. The city was the seat of his new government. Manco escaped and headed an unsuccessful uprising. Two or three years later Pizarro and Almagro quarreled about the territory each was to govern. This contest soon assumed the proportions of a civil war. Pizarro's supporters captured and executed Almagro. The embittered and discontented followers of Almagro then conspired against Pizarro. They assassinated him in Lima on June 26, 1541.

CHAPTER 12

PÁNFILO DE NARVÁEZ

The Spanish soldier and adventurer Pánfilo de Narváez took part in the expedition that conquered Cuba. He was also one of the earliest European explorers of Florida.

Narváez was born in about 1478 in Valladolid, Spain. As a young man, he entered military service and became one of the first Spanish settlers of Jamaica. In 1511 he commanded a company of archers in Diego Velásquez's campaign to conquer and pacify Cuba. As a reward, Narváez was appointed to public offices and given large tracts of land on Cuba. In 1520 he was sent to capture and replace Hernán Cortés as ruler of Mexico. Narváez was defeated and held prisoner by Cortés for two years.

In 1526 the Spanish king gave Narváez permission to colonize the land from Florida westward. He set sail the following year. He reached Florida, claimed the land for Spain, and began leading his men through the interior, fighting Indians along the way. Narváez was lost at sea in November 1528 while attempting to sail to Mexico. Only a few of his men survived; among them was Álvar Núñez Cabeza de Vaca, who wandered through what is now Texas for some eight years.

CHAPTER 13

HERNANDO DE SOTO

One of the most famous gold seekers in history was Hernando de Soto. He was born in about 1496 in Jerez de los Caballeros, Spain. In 1514 he sailed to the New World with Pedro Arias Dávila, governor of Darién (now Panama). He became a ruthless soldier whose men feared his temper but admired his horsemanship.

In 1524 and 1526 he took part in expeditions to Central America. In 1532 he joined Francisco Pizarro in the conquest of Peru. De Soto's share of the Peruvian treasures made him rich. He returned to Spain and married Dávila's daughter Isabel.

The Spaniards did not know the country north of Florida. Captive Indians told stories of lands there richer than Mexico or Peru. De Soto decided to win another fortune from this region. He persuaded the king of Spain to appoint him governor of Cuba and Florida. He recruited a thousand men and helped pay for their equipment. This great army set sail from Spain in April 1538. At Havana they set up an advance base and made final preparations.

Hernando de Soto. Encyclopædia Britannica, Inc.

On May 30, 1539, de Soto and his men went ashore at Tampa Bay in Florida. They marched northward to Georgia, then turned westward and followed the Alabama River to Mobile Bay. When their supplies and spirits ran low, de Soto rallied his men with the prospect of riches ahead.

Along the way they met many Indian tribes. De Soto forced the Indians to furnish supplies and tortured their chiefs in a useless effort to make them tell where gold was hidden. This brutality led to many battles. The bloodiest was fought near Mobile Bay. About 70 Spaniards were killed, and many more were hurt. De Soto himself was severely wounded.

De Soto first saw the Mississippi River near the present site of Memphis, Tenn., in the spring of 1541. De Soto's men built boats and crossed the Mississippi River. By the next autumn they reached the Neosho River in northeastern Oklahoma before they turned eastward again.

Everywhere de Soto searched, the Indians reported gold "just ahead" in order to escape his torture, but after three years he still had found no gold. In the spring of 1542 de Soto led his worn and tattered men southward. Near the junction of the Red and the Mississippi rivers, de Soto fell ill and died.

CHAPTER 14

FRANCISCO VÁZQUEZ DE CORONADO

One of the strangest journeys ever made in search of gold was led by the Spaniard Francisco Vázquez de Coronado. His army of several hundred Spaniards, Indians, and slaves was accompanied by herds of cattle, pigs, and sheep. Instead of the cities filled with treasure that he expected to find in the wilderness north of Mexico, Coronado found only poor Indian villages. He did, however, establish Spain's later claim to land that now covers a huge portion of the United States. The claim stretched from what is now California into Oklahoma and Kansas.

Coronado was born to a noble family of Salamanca, Spain, in about 1510. As a young man at court he became friendly with Antonio de Mendoza, one of the king's favorites. Mendoza was appointed viceroy of New Spain (Mexico) in 1535, and Coronado went with him to America. In Mexico City Coronado married wealthy Beatriz Estrada. In 1538 Mendoza appointed Coronado governor of New Galicia, a province in western Mexico.

Francisco Vázquez de Coronado crosses the plains of Kansas on his 1541 expedition to conquer the Seven Golden Cities of Cibola. **MPI/Archive Photos/Getty Images**

Explorers brought back stories of the Seven Golden Cities of Cibola. Mendoza made Coronado the commander of an expedition to seize the treasure. Coronado led his party from Culiacán, a northern outpost of New Galicia, in April 1540. The expedition came upon the first of the promised seven cities in July. The golden cities of Cibola were actually the Indian pueblos of present-day

Zuñi in western New Mexico. From here Coronado sent out scouting parties. One discovered the Grand Canyon. Another found more pueblos in a fertile area of the Rio Grande valley.

Here the expedition spent the winter. New hope came when an Indian slave told of a new land to the northeast whose capital, Quivira, was very rich. With 30 men and the slave as guide, Coronado set forth. After months they found Quivira in what is now central Kansas. It held only Indian tepees. The slave confessed he had invented the story and was executed. Coronado returned to the Rio Grande.

After spending a second winter in the pueblos, the expedition started homeward. The tattered army followed a route over deserts and mountains in blazing summer heat. In the fall of 1542 Coronado led only about 100 men into Mexico City. The remaining survivors trailed in during the next months. In 1544, during an official inquiry, Coronado was charged with corruption and negligence and removed as governor of New Galicia. He returned to Mexico City, where he retained his post as an alderman until he died on September 22, 1554.

CHAPTER 15

JACQUES CARTIER

In the early 1500s French explorer Jacques Cartier tried to find a sea passage to the East Indies through North America. Instead he discovered the St. Lawrence River and opened Canada to European settlement.

Cartier was born in St-Malo, France, on December 31, 1491. Very little is known of his early life. On the first of his voyages to North America he set sail from St-Malo on April 20, 1534. On May 10 he reached northern Newfoundland. He passed through the Strait of Belle Isle and explored the Gulf of St. Lawrence.

On May 16, 1535, Cartier sailed again from France. This time he had three vessels. He camped at a spot, far up the St. Lawrence, that the Indians called Stadacona, near the present site of Quebec. He took his smallest ship and two boats up the river to where it widens into Lake St. Peter. There his ship went aground on shoals. Cartier then continued his exploration in small boats and on foot. He reached the fortified Indian village of Hochelaga on an island where the Ottawa and St. Lawrence rivers meet. He gave the name Mont Réal (Mount Royal) to the highest hill on the island. The city of Montreal now occupies the site.

Cartier went up the river until stopped by the Lachine Rapids. He wintered at Stadacona, where 25 of his 110 men died of scurvy. In the spring, with 12 captured Indians, he returned to France.

In 1541 he took colonists in five ships to Cap Rouge, near Quebec. He returned to France in 1542. The colony was a failure, and for the time being France lost interest in Canada. Cartier retired to St-Malo, where he served as an adviser on navigation. He died on September 1, 1557.

CHAPTER 16

SIR FRANCIS DRAKE

The first Englishman to sail around the world was Sir Francis Drake. He also took a leading part in defeating the Great Armada sent by Spain to invade England.

Born near Tavistock, in Devonshire, Drake grew up in a seafaring atmosphere. While still a boy he worked as a sailor. When he was 20 he sailed with his cousin, Sir John Hawkins, to Guinea on the west coast of Africa to obtain slaves. He rose to command a ship under Hawkins and was with him when Spaniards attacked the fleet off the port of Veracruz in Mexico. All but two of the English ships were destroyed in this battle, and Drake lost nearly everything he possessed. Drake never forgave the Spanish for their treachery on this occasion or for their cruel treatment of their English prisoners. He devoted the rest of his life to a relentless war against Spain.

Drake gathered together his own band of adventurers and made three profitable voyages to the New World, plundering Spanish settlements and destroying Spanish ships. In 1572 he made a daring march across the

Illustration of Sir Francis Drake, circa 1585. Stock Montage/Archive Photos/Getty Images

Isthmus of Panama. From a high tree he caught his first glimpse of the Pacific Ocean.

Drake's great voyage around the world, between 1577 and 1580, had the secret financial support of Queen Elizabeth I and the war party in her council. They hoped it would end the Spanish monopoly of the profitable trade in the Pacific. Drake set out sailing with five ships. He intended to pass through the Strait of Magellan, at the southern tip of South America, and then explore the waters he had seen from the Isthmus of Panama. When the straits were passed, Drake's ship, the *Golden Hind*, pushed on alone, the other vessels having either turned back or been lost. As he went up the coast, he plundered Spanish settlements in Chile and Peru and captured treasure ships bound for Panama.

Drake then sailed northward and claimed the California coast in the name of his queen. To avoid meeting the angered Spaniards by returning the way he came, he determined to return home by sailing around the world, as Ferdinand Magellan had done. He crossed the Pacific and Indian oceans and reached the Atlantic by sailing around the southern tip of Africa. He reached England in September 1580, nearly three years after he set out. He was warmly acclaimed. Elizabeth shared the treasure he brought on his ship, which was "literally ballasted with silver." She honored him by dining on board his ship and by raising him to knighthood, though she knew this would infuriate the Spaniards.

In the war with Spain that broke out in 1585, Drake won his crowning honors. After once more carrying death and destruction to Spanish settlements in the West Indies, he led a daring expedition into the port of Cádiz, Spain. Here he destroyed so many vessels that for an entire year the Spaniards had to delay the expedition they were preparing for the invasion of England. Drake returned home in triumph.

When the Spanish Armada finally did come sailing up the English Channel in 1588, Drake, as vice admiral of the English fleet, played a chief role in the week-long running fight that drove off the Spaniards. During the fighting Drake encountered a galleon commanded by Don Pedro de Valdez. Don Pedro was one of the leading promoters of the idea of dispatching the Armada to England. Yet when he and his men learned that their

An engraving shows Sir Francis Drake's fleet in the port of Santo Domingo on the island of Hispaniola during England's war with Spain in 1585. Buyenlarge/Archive Photos/Getty Images

opponent was the daring El Draque (the dragon) they surrendered at once.

Some eight years later, on a final expedition against the Spaniards in the West Indies, Drake became ill and died on board his ship in January 1596 off the coast of Panama. More than any other of England's bold privateers, he had helped to set England on the way to becoming the mistress of the seas.

CHAPTER 17

SIR WALTER RALEIGH

Politician and poet, soldier and sailor, explorer and historian, Walter Raleigh exemplifies the many-sided genius demonstrated by a number of notable men and women during the reign of Queen Elizabeth I. His heroic activities typify the bold imagination and adventurous life of the era. Raleigh's principal claim to fame, however, rests on his efforts to colonize the New World. His dream of establishing a new England beyond the Atlantic sustained him through years of disappointment.

Early Life

Raleigh was born at Hayes Barton, Devonshire, in about 1554. In 1569 he went to France, where he fought on the side of the Huguenots (or French Protestants) in that country's wars of religion. He later attended Oriel College, Oxford, and Middle Temple, a law school in London. In 1580 his participation in the suppression of the

Irish rebellion in Munster attracted attention, and soon afterward he was introduced at court, where he became a favorite of Elizabeth I. A famous story about Raleigh tells how he won the queen's favor by placing his velvet cloak over a muddy spot in her path so that she could walk over it without soiling her shoes.

Raleigh's tall and handsome figure, his dark hair, lofty forehead, resolute bearing, courtly manners, and spirited wit all combined to form an imposing personality. But he could also be haughty, and because his pride and impatience made him many enemies he was never fully admitted to the queen's counsels in matters of state. The playful name of Water that she applied to him would indicate that she recognized the instability of character that was his great fault and that in the end brought about his ruin. Elizabeth, however, lavished numerous favors upon him throughout her reign. He was awarded large properties in Ireland and in 1585 was knighted. In return he discharged with conspicuous ability the responsibilities of several important positions to which she appointed him.

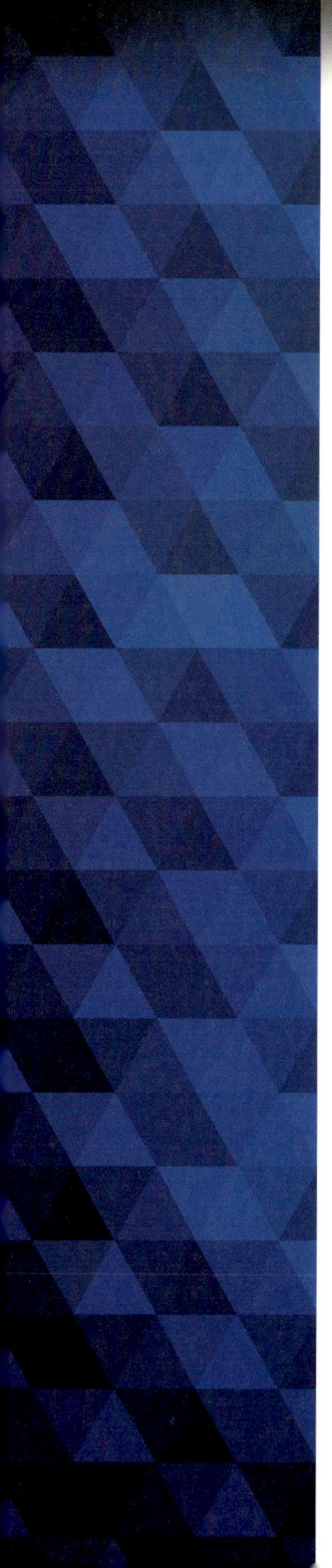

Expeditions

Before his appearance at court Raleigh had gone on voyages of discovery with his half brother, Sir Humphrey Gilbert. Up to that time the English had made no permanent settlements in America. Raleigh's position at court gave him an opportunity to press for this project, though the queen would not let him lead any of his colonizing expeditions in person.

Tireless in his efforts to establish an English colony in America, Raleigh sent out expedition after expedition. The name Virginia—in honor of the Virgin Queen, as Elizabeth was called—was given to the area explored in 1584 by one of these expeditions. Three settlements were made on islands off the North Carolina coast, but none survived.

Raleigh's pioneering work paved the way for later settlements in the New World. When some of his followers returned to England, they brought back tobacco from America. By popularizing its use Raleigh created a demand for the tobacco leaf, which became a profitable crop in the colonies. He also helped introduce tobacco and potatoes in Ireland.

Sir Walter Raleigh burns down the town of Saint Joseph, then the capital of Spanish Trinidad. **FPG/Archive Photos/Getty Images**

In 1595 Raleigh headed an exploring expedition to the Guiana region on the north coast of South America in search of the fabled El Dorado, the legendary ruler of a region abounding in gold and jewels. His trip was unsuccessful, and after much hardship he returned home empty-handed. He recounted his adventures in a book published in

1596, *The Discoverie of Guiana*. In the same year he took part in an expedition against Cádiz, Spain.

Imprisonment and Death

Raleigh's popularity at court had begun to decline when the queen found out about his secret marriage to one of her maids of honor, Elizabeth Throckmorton. When Elizabeth I died and James I came to the throne, Raleigh's situation quickly grew worse. The Scottish king, suspecting that Raleigh had worked against his becoming king of England, revoked Raleigh's numerous offices and privileges.

In July 1603 Raleigh was arrested and sent to the Tower of London. After a grossly unfair trial he was condemned to death for conspiring against the king's life. His gallant bearing turned public opinion in his favor, however, and the death sentence was suspended. During the 13 years he spent as a prisoner in the Tower, his wife and son were often permitted to live with him, and he was visited by many great scholars and poets. He worked on a book, *The History of the World*, for King James's son, Prince Henry, whose favor he enjoyed. Only one volume of this vast project was finished. Raleigh also wrote on political philosophy and was a skillful poet.

In 1616 Raleigh finally persuaded King James to release him so that he might lead an expedition to the Orinoco River and bring back gold from a mine he claimed to have discovered. Disobeying the king's orders, Raleigh's men fought the Spaniards while he was incapacitated by a severe fever. Raleigh returned empty-handed to face the protests of Spain.

King James, who wanted to remain on good terms with Spain, arrested him once again. Raleigh was executed in 1618 under his old sentence, which had never been revoked. Cheerful and resolute to the last, he asked to see the ax when he was led to the scaffold. Touching the edge, he said, "This is a sharp medicine, but it is a sure cure for all diseases." Raleigh died on October 29, 1618, in London.

CHAPTER 18

SAMUEL DE CHAMPLAIN

Called the Father of New France, Samuel de Champlain founded Quebec, the first permanent French settlement in North America. He also kept the struggling community alive during its early years. He explored New France (France's possessions in North America) as far west as Lake Huron and also discovered the lake in New York that bears his name.

Samuel de Champlain was born in 1567 in Brouage, a small French seaport on the Bay of Biscay. His father was a sea captain, and young Champlain was trained in seamanship, navigation, and mapmaking.

Champlain gained a reputation as a fine navigator when he commanded a two-year voyage to the West Indies and Mexico. His report on his visits to the principal Spanish ports in Central America impressed King Henry IV, who made him the royal geographer. For supplying the first real information the French had about the Spanish possessions, Champlain was also granted the title of *sieur*.

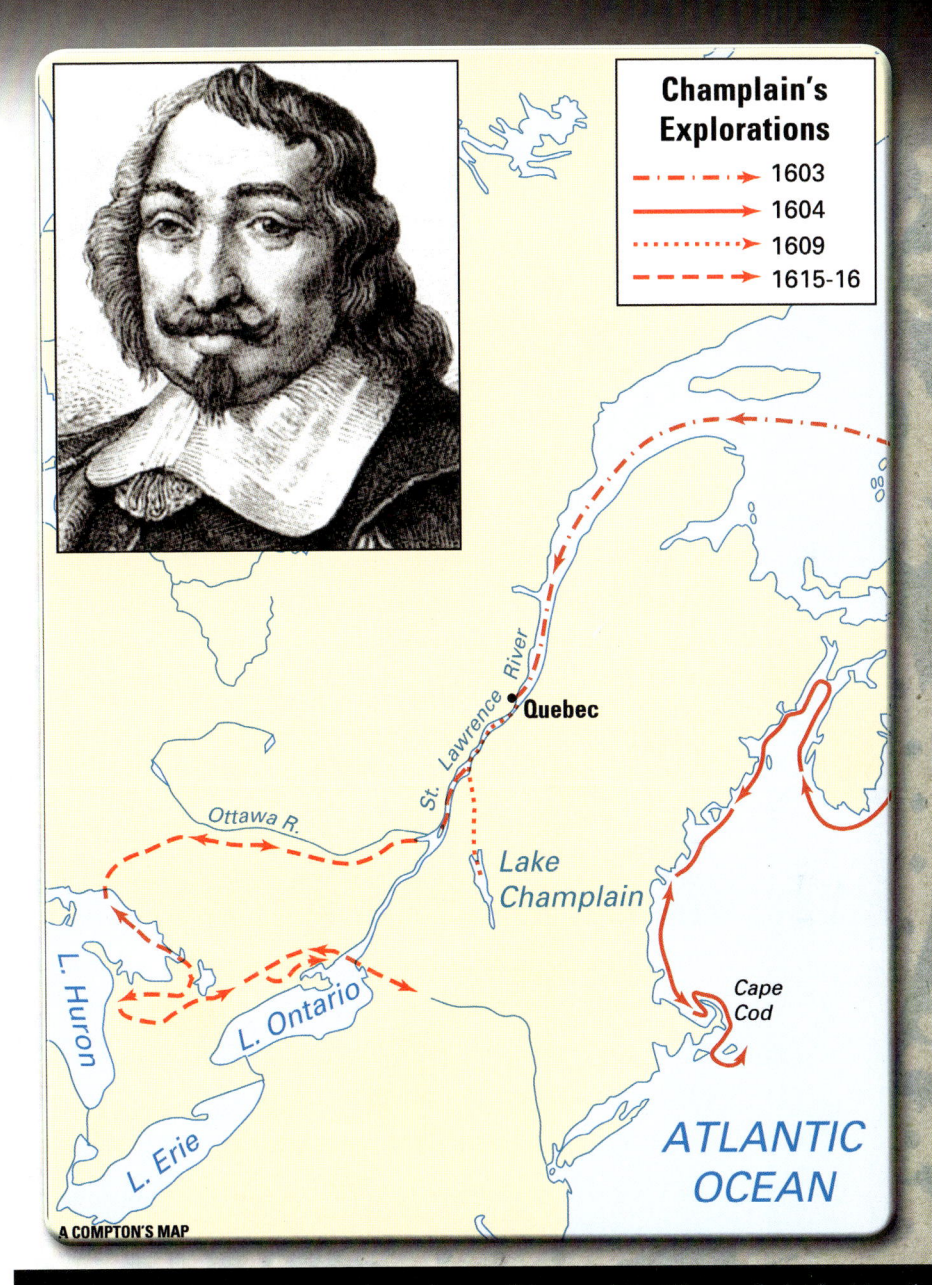

Champlain's Explorations
- 1603
- 1604
- 1609
- 1615-16

Map depicting the explorations of Samuel de Champlain in North America in the early 17th century.

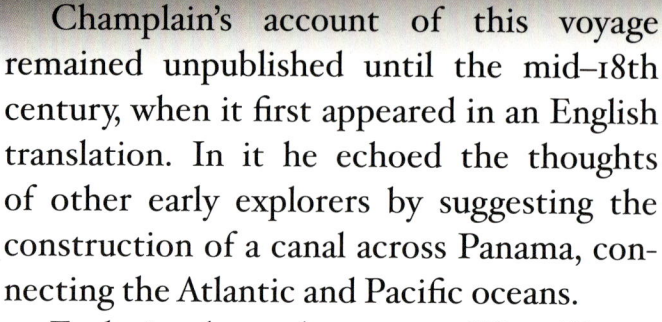

Champlain's account of this voyage remained unpublished until the mid–18th century, when it first appeared in an English translation. In it he echoed the thoughts of other early explorers by suggesting the construction of a canal across Panama, connecting the Atlantic and Pacific oceans.

Early in the 17th century, King Henry granted Pierre de Monts, a nobleman, a fur-trading monopoly in New France. In return, de Monts agreed to establish colonies there. Champlain, who explored the St. Lawrence River for the first time in 1603, returned to New France in 1604 with a group of colonists under the command of de Monts. The settlers built dwellings and a storehouse on Dochet Island near the mouth of the St. Croix River. After a hard winter they moved across the Bay of Fundy to a better site in what is now Nova Scotia. Champlain spent two years in the region, and during that time he explored the Atlantic coast as far south as Cape Cod.

In 1608 Champlain was granted permission to lead another expedition. He led a group of settlers to a site on the St. Lawrence River where they hoped to establish a center for controlling the fur trade. There he founded Quebec and made friends of the Huron people of the region. In 1609 he went with the Huron to fight the Iroquois in New York. During this time he came upon Lake Champlain. Not far from the lake, on July 30, he routed the enemy with gunfire. Thereafter the Iroquois were bitter enemies of the French.

Champlain then made several exploring trips, seeking rivers that might lead to the Pacific Ocean. In 1615 he reached Georgian Bay and Lake Huron. After 1616 he acted as leader in Quebec and visited France often, seeking help.

In 1629 Champlain was taken to England as a prisoner after the British seized Quebec. He was released in 1632, and the colony was returned to France. In 1633 Champlain returned to Quebec as governor. He died there on December 25, 1635.

CHAPTER 19

HENRY HUDSON

Because of the thriving trade in spices and silk between Asia and Europe, Henry Hudson and other explorers made a number of difficult and dangerous voyages searching for a northeast or northwest passage. Such a passage would provide a shorter, quicker way to the Pacific. Explorers sought a shortcut northward from the east coast of Europe and thence either eastward over the top of Europe and Asia or westward over the top of North America. Hudson tried both routes. Although he did not succeed, his four voyages added greatly to knowledge of the Arctic and North America.

Little is known of Hudson before 1607, when he undertook the first of two voyages for the English Muscovy Company. He sailed to Greenland and searched vainly for a passage through the polar ice barrier around the Svalbard archipelago. On a second voyage, in 1608, Hudson reached Novaya Zemlya, islands north of Russia, but again he was turned back by ice.

The next year, in command of the *Half Moon* for the Dutch East India Company,

Engraving of the Robert Weir painting **The Landing Of Hendrick Hudson,** *illustrating Henry Hudson's greeting by Native Americans in the early 1600s.* **Stock Montage/Archive Photos/Getty Images**

Hudson sailed to North America. He explored the inlets southward along the coast to southern Virginia, probing for a passage across the continent. He then turned northward and entered the Hudson River, which is now named after him. He sailed upstream to the vicinity of what is now Albany, N.Y.

A group of Englishmen backed Hudson's fourth voyage in 1610–11. With the *Discovery* and a crew of 25 men, Hudson sailed into what is now Hudson Bay and explored the east coast to its southernmost reach in James Bay. After a winter caught in the ice, the *Discovery* sailed northward. Again it was icebound. Most of the crew mutinied. On June 22, 1611, Hudson, his son, and seven sick men were forced into a small boat and left to freeze or starve. The mutineers headed home, but several of their leaders were killed by Eskimo. The rest reached England, where they were tried for mutiny but found not guilty.

CHAPTER 20

JACQUES MARQUETTE

Traveling with his fellow adventurer Louis Jolliet, the French explorer and missionary Father Jacques Marquette explored the upper Mississippi River and reported the first accurate data on its course. The story of the long and dangerous journey of Marquette and Jolliet is one of the most interesting chapters in the history of the exploration of the New World.

Marquette was born on June 1, 1637, in Laon, France. By nature a thoughtful and gentle person, he decided at the age of 17 to become a Jesuit priest. For several years after entering the priesthood, he taught at Jesuit schools in northern France. All this time he hoped that he would become a missionary overseas.

In 1666 Marquette's wish was granted. His superiors sent him to Quebec in New France (now part of Canada). There he studied Indian languages, and in 1668 he was appointed to a mission among the Ottawa Indians at Sault Ste. Marie (now in Michigan). The first winter, 1668–69, was comparatively comfortable. During this time he first met the young French Canadian explorer Louis Jolliet.

Marquette left the mission in September 1669 to go to La Pointe mission in the Apostle Islands of Lake Superior. During the 18 months he spent there, he was visited by a group of Illinois Indians and wanted to establish a mission among them. His Indian friends told him of the great river they had crossed to reach him. A quarrel with the Sioux Indians forced Marquette's converts to flee to Lake Michigan in 1671. Marquette accompanied them. That summer he founded the mission of St. Ignace on the north shore of the Straits of Mackinac.

Jolliet came to St. Ignace in December 1672. The governor of New France, the Count de Frontenac, had commissioned him to find the great river of which the Indians spoke. Marquette was to be his companion. All through the winter the two men made their preparations. On May 17, 1673, the expedition got under way. It consisted of Marquette, Jolliet, and five other men. The entire party traveled in two birchbark canoes.

They paddled down Green Bay into the Fox River. Traveling up the Fox, they portaged (carried their canoes) to the head

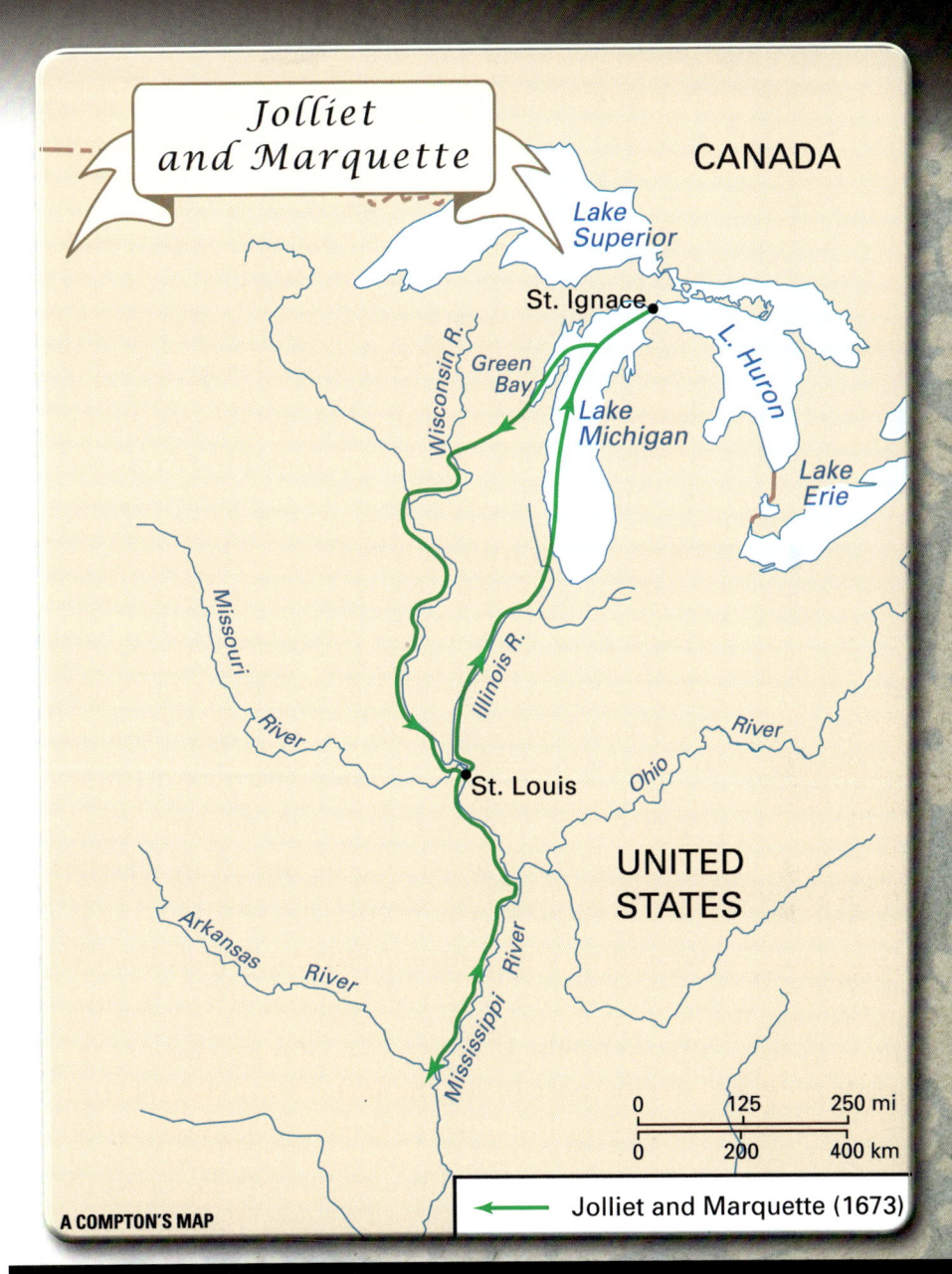

Map depicting the expedition of Jolliet and Marquette in North America in 1673.

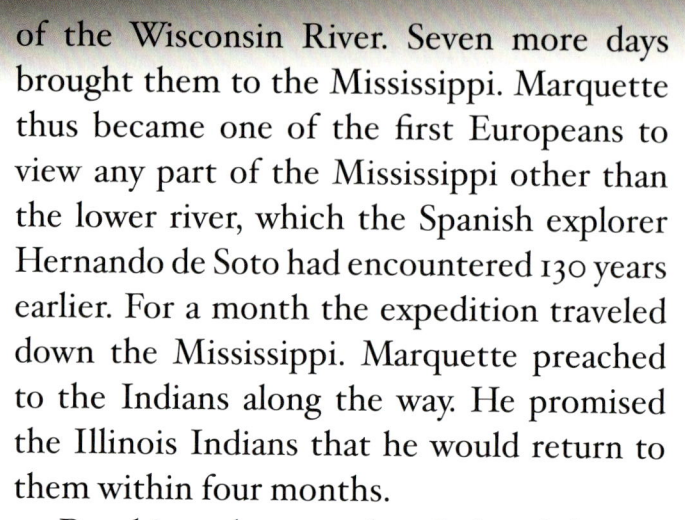

of the Wisconsin River. Seven more days brought them to the Mississippi. Marquette thus became one of the first Europeans to view any part of the Mississippi other than the lower river, which the Spanish explorer Hernando de Soto had encountered 130 years earlier. For a month the expedition traveled down the Mississippi. Marquette preached to the Indians along the way. He promised the Illinois Indians that he would return to them within four months.

Reaching the mouth of the Arkansas River, they learned that the Mississippi eventually flowed into the Gulf of Mexico (and not into the Pacific Ocean as they had hoped). They also found out that if they continued on the river they would run into Spanish territory. Having learned the location of the river's mouth, the explorers turned back. Reaching the Illinois River, they followed its course into the Des Plaines River. A portage brought them to the Chicago River and Lake Michigan. In the last days of September they came to rest at the little mission of St. Francis Xavier at De Pere, near the head of Green Bay.

In less than five months the expedition had traveled more than 2,500 miles (4,000 kilometers). Marquette's health had suffered greatly. He remained at De Pere for more than a year, writing his journal as he recovered. Then in October 1674 he set out to found a mission among the Illinois Indians.

The trip proved fatal for the frail Marquette. He and his two companions were forced to spend the winter at a camp they set up at the mouth of the Chicago River. Parties of Illinois Indians visited them. By the end of March, Marquette thought himself well enough to continue on to the Indian village on the shore of the Illinois River. There he preached on Easter, speaking to a large audience. His health, however, grew worse. Marquette tried to return to his mission at St. Ignace, but he collapsed and died on the way, on May 18, 1675, at the mouth of the river now known as Père Marquette (meaning "Father Marquette"), at what is now Ludington, Mich.

CHAPTER 21

LOUIS JOLLIET

The French Canadian explorer Louis Jolliet traveled the upper Mississippi River in 1673 along with the French Jesuit missionary Jacques Marquette. They were the first people of European descent to explore the river's upper reaches; the Spaniard Hernando de Soto had explored the lower Mississippi in 1541.

Jolliet was born before September 21, 1645, probably in Beaupré, near the city of Quebec, Canada. He studied for the priesthood at the Jesuit seminary in Quebec. Before taking the final vows he changed his mind and went to France for a year's study in science.

Back in Canada, Jolliet worked as a fur trader, traveling through the wilderness around the Great Lakes. He became an expert mapmaker and was skilled in Indian languages. In 1672 the Count de Frontenac, governor of New France, selected Jolliet and Marquette to find the great river in the west. At that time the river—the Mississippi—was known to French Canadians only by rumor.

Jolliet, Marquette, and five other men set out on May 17, 1673, in two birchbark canoes.

They traveled from what is now St. Ignace, Mich., to Green Bay and continued up the Fox River and down the Wisconsin River. After about a month, they entered the Mississippi River. They reached a Quapaw Indian village at the mouth of the Arkansas River, in what is now Arkansas, in July. Learning that the Mississippi River empties into the Gulf of Mexico, in what was then Spanish territory, the men decided to return home.

During their journey Jolliet's maps and papers were lost when his canoe tipped over. Marquette's account of the expedition was of help to the French explorer La Salle, however, who explored the Mississippi to its mouth at the Gulf of Mexico in 1682.

Jolliet was granted the feudal rights to several islands in the lower St. Lawrence River. After his marriage in 1675 he established his home on Anticosti Island. He made further explorations for New France and was appointed royal cartographer. He died in the summer of 1700 in what is now the province of Quebec.

CHAPTER 22

SIEUR DE LA SALLE

The father of the great Louisiana Territory was the French explorer René-Robert Cavelier, sieur de La Salle. He was the first European to voyage down the Mississippi River to the Gulf of Mexico. As a result of this exploration France laid claim to the entire Mississippi Valley under the name of Louisiana.

Early Life

René-Robert Cavelier was born on November 22, 1643, in Rouen, France. The son of a rich merchant, he was educated by the Jesuits. When he was 23 years old he sailed for Montreal, Canada, to seek his fortune. He got a grant of land at Lachine (now part of Montreal) from the Seminary of St. Sulpice, where his older brother was a priest. He was more interested, however, in Montreal's greatest activity, the fur trade, than he was in farming.

La Salle set up a fur-trading post and farmed his land. He soon learned the

René-Robert Cavelier, sieur de La Salle. **Encyclopædia Britannica, Inc.**

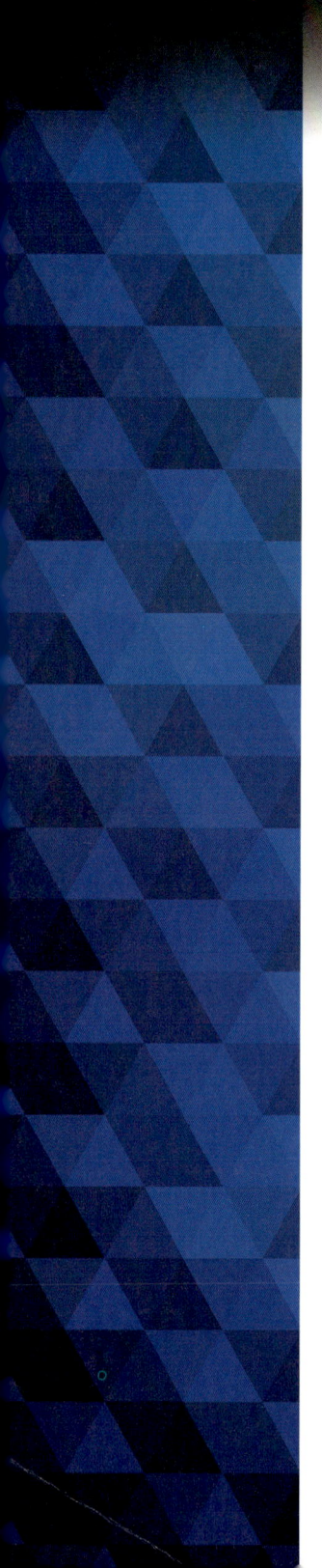

Iroquoian language and several other Indian dialects. From the Indians he heard that south of the Great Lakes a broad river ran southwest to "the Vermilion Sea." La Salle thought that this sea might be the Gulf of California. If so, "the great river" would be a splendid route to China.

La Salle sold his land to finance an expedition in 1669–70. He ascended the St. Lawrence River to Lake Ontario. His men paddled along the southern shore until they came to the west end of the lake. The records of his exploration from here on were lost. Upon his return he found the Count de Frontenac in power.

Attempts to Expand New France

In 1673 Louis Jolliet and Jacques Marquette had explored the Mississippi far enough to prove that the river emptied into the Gulf of Mexico. Frontenac and La Salle at once proposed to build a chain of forts and trading posts along the Great Lakes and the Mississippi to hold the region and its fur trade for France. The French wanted this protection because the Iroquois Indians were trying to force the fur trade through New York into the hands of their allies, the Dutch and English traders at Albany.

Frontenac had made a start on this plan by building Fort Frontenac (1673), where the St. Lawrence flows out of Lake Ontario, at what is now Kingston, Ont. La Salle was to be made governor of the West and given a monopoly of trade in the region. In return, he was to build and maintain the needed forts. La Salle made two trips to France, in 1674 and 1677, before he received the monopoly and was given his title of *sieur* ("lord," in English).

In the winter of 1678–79 an advance party built a fort at the Niagara River and started to build a 40-ton ship, the *Griffon*. On August 7, 1679, La Salle and his lieutenant, Henri de Tonty, started for Green Bay on the first voyage ever made by a ship on the Great Lakes.

La Salle and Tonty reached Green Bay in September and sent the ship back laden with furs. In December 1679 they established Fort Miami at what is now St. Joseph, Mich. Early in 1680 La Salle built Fort Crèvecoeur ("heartbreak") near the site of present-day Peoria, Ill. From this fort he sent Father Louis Hennepin with two companions to explore the upper Mississippi.

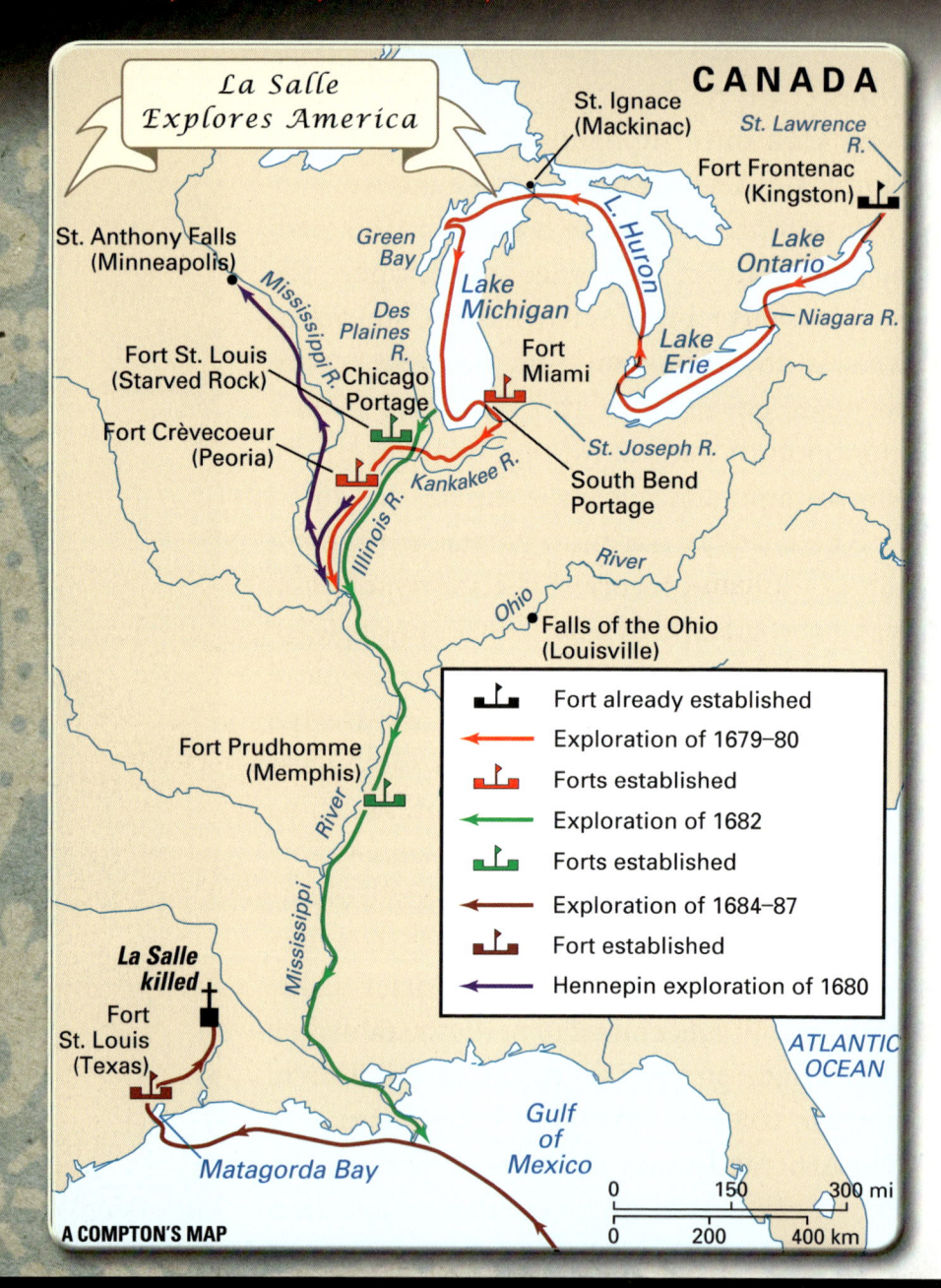

Map depicting La Salle's explorations in North Americain the late 17th century.

Leaving Tonty in charge of the new fort, La Salle made a fast trip back to Fort Frontenac, where he found out that the *Griffon* never had been heard from. On his return westward, he learned that the Iroquois had ravaged the country. Fort Crèvecoeur was in ashes. Tonty and his men had vanished. La Salle traced him northward to what is now Mackinaw City, Mich. The veteran had fought his way out through the Green Bay region.

La Salle now spent a year organizing the Illinois Indians to resist the Iroquois. Early in 1682 the explorer followed the Illinois River and the Mississippi to the Gulf of Mexico. On April 9 he named the entire Mississippi Valley "Louisiana" and claimed it for France. Retracing his steps, La Salle built Fort St. Louis at Starved Rock, Ill., and organized a colony of Illinois Indians.

In 1683 he sought help from Quebec to maintain the new colony. However, he found that Frontenac had been recalled and his own rights had been canceled by the new governor. He went to France and persuaded King Louis XIV to renew his rights and to help him procure four ships and about 400 men for a post at the mouth of the Mississippi.

Final Expedition

This expedition by sea ruined La Salle. The naval commander, Beaujeu, who had charge of the ships, opposed him constantly. In the West Indies, La Salle fell sick. Many men deserted. When the explorer set sail again with only about 180 men, he lost his way. Finally, he landed at Matagorda Bay, Tex., where Beaujeu left him with one small ship on March 12, 1685.

La Salle started to build a second Fort St. Louis and scouted for the Mississippi. His ship was wrecked, and he lost all but 36 of his men. In January 1687 he took half the men on an overland trip in an attempt to reach Tonty in Illinois. On March 19 near the Brazos River in eastern Texas, three of his men murdered him.

CHAPTER 23

JAMES COOK

The English navigator Captain James Cook became an explorer because of his love of adventure and curiosity about distant lands and their people. He surveyed a greater length of coastline than any other explorer and remade the map of the Pacific. His voyages gave Britain the lands now occupied by Australia and New Zealand.

James Cook was born in Marton, Yorkshire, in 1728. His father was a farmer. Apprenticed at 12 to a haberdasher and later to a shipowner, in 1755 he joined the Royal Navy. Four years later, as master of the ship *Mercury*, he took part in expeditions against the French in the St. Lawrence River.

His skill in sounding, surveying, and charting this river won for him the post of marine surveyor of the coasts of Newfoundland and Labrador. He published books of sailing directions that showed remarkable abilities. He also won a reputation as astronomer and mathematician by his account of a solar eclipse off the coast of North America.

In 1768 Cook was put in command of the ship *Endeavour* to observe a transit of the planet Venus in the South Pacific. He spent six months circumnavigating and mapping the coasts of New Zealand. From New Zealand he proceeded to the east coast of Australia. Cook named the east coast New South Wales because he thought it resembled the south coast of Wales in Britain. The naturalists who accompanied him named a bay, near the present site of Sydney, Botany Bay because of the richness of the vegetation growing there. After exploring the coast of New Guinea, Cook returned to England in 1771.

Cook's second voyage, from 1772 to 1775, was undertaken to prove or disprove that there was a great continent in the southern Pacific Ocean, to the southeast of Australia. He crossed the Antarctic Circle—the first European to do this—but did not go far enough south to discover the true Antarctic continent. From west to east he explored the entire far southern Pacific, mapping known islands and discovering several new ones. The maps he made of this region differ little in their main outlines from those in use today. On his return home, he received the Copley medal for his success in preventing scurvy by feeding his sailors sauerkraut juice.

A cutaway painting of Captain Cook's ship Endeavour. **Robert W. Nicholson/National Geographic Image Collection/Getty Images**

At 48 Cook was still eager for adventure. In 1776 he set out on his third voyage to settle the question of a possible sea passage across America or around it to the north—the so-called Northwest Passage. He came upon the Hawaiian Islands, which had been discovered earlier by the Spanish, and named them the Sandwich Islands in honor of the earl of Sandwich, first lord of the Admiralty.

Cook made extensive explorations of the northwestern coast of North America, seeking an inlet. Beyond Bering Strait he found that a solid wall of ice blocked the passage. Forced to turn back, he returned to Hawaii. He had won the friendship of the people there by his wise and kind treatment. Trouble arose, however, when one of the ship's boats was stolen. Cook took some men ashore to recover the boat. A scuffle followed in which he was killed.

CHAPTER 24

DAVID THOMPSON

When a monument was unveiled in Castlegar, B.C., in 1954 to commemorate David Thompson's exploration of the Columbia River, he was called "Canada's Greatest Geographer." He was the first man to explore and chart the Columbia from its source in the Selkirk Mountains to its mouth in the Pacific Ocean. In the course of 25 years he traveled some 50,000 miles (80,000 kilometers) in western Canada and the northwestern United States. He also mapped water and land routes of travel covering an area of 1.7 million square miles (4.4 million square kilometers).

David Thompson was born on April 30, 1770, in London, England. His father died when the boy was 2 years old. At 14 he went to Canada to join the Hudson's Bay Company as an apprentice in the fur trade. He was assigned to work with Samuel Hearne, an explorer, and Philip Turnor, a surveyor. They taught him mathematics and the use of surveying instruments. He decided to become a surveyor.

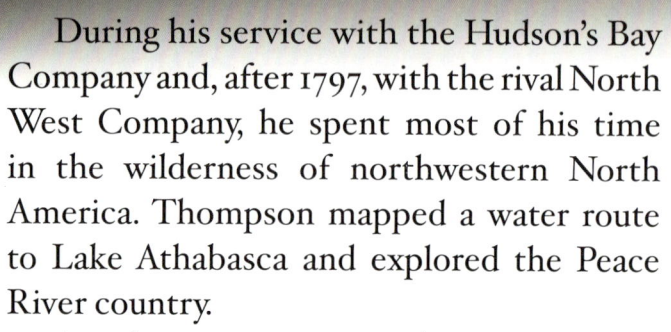

During his service with the Hudson's Bay Company and, after 1797, with the rival North West Company, he spent most of his time in the wilderness of northwestern North America. Thompson mapped a water route to Lake Athabasca and explored the Peace River country.

Another survey covered territory from Lake Winnipegosis on the north to sources of the Mississippi River on the south and the course of the St. Louis River to Lake Superior. Meanwhile he traded with the Indians, established fur-trading posts, and made charts and observations wherever he went. In 1811 he charted the length of the Columbia River.

In 1812 Thompson retired from field service and spent two years making a great map of western Canada and the northwestern United States. This map formed the basis for all future maps of western Canada. It is now in the Archives of Ontario, in Toronto.

From 1816 to 1826 Thompson was in charge of establishing and marking part of the boundary between Canada and the United States. After 10 more years of public and private surveying, he retired to Williamstown, Ont. In 1799 he had married Charlotte Small, and they had 13 children. After his retirement Thompson's sons failed in business, losing their father's investment. Thompson then moved to Longueuil, near Montreal, Que. His eyesight failed, and he became destitute. He died on February 10, 1857, in Longueuil. In 1916 the Champlain Society published some of his records under the title *David Thompson's Narrative of His Explorations in Western America*.

CHAPTER 25

MERIWETHER LEWIS

The name of Meriwether Lewis is closely linked with that of another American explorer, William Clark. Together they led the Lewis and Clark Expedition of 1804–06.

Early Life

Lewis was born on August 18, 1774, on a plantation near Charlottesville, Va. Thomas Jefferson, a neighbor, was a friend of the family. Lewis studied with private tutors, hunted, and learned nature lore. In 1794 he served in the militia during the Whiskey Rebellion. The next year he fought against Native Americans in the Northwest Territory. Between campaigns he lived in the wilderness and learned Native American languages and customs.

Soon after Jefferson became U.S. president, Lewis became his private secretary. In 1803 Jefferson appointed Lewis commander of an expedition to explore the

Meriwether Lewis, portrait by Charles Willson Peale; in Independence National Historical Park, Philadelphia. Courtesy of the Independence National Historical Park Collection, Philadelphia

American territory newly acquired from France in the Louisiana Purchase. Lewis chose his friend William Clark to be his companion officer. In the winter of 1803–04 the expedition was assembled in Illinois, near St. Louis. The group, called the Corps of Discovery, originally consisted of about four dozen men.

The Expedition

On May 14, 1804, the explorers started up the Missouri River in a 55-foot (17-meter) covered keelboat and two small canoes. On August 3 they held their first meeting with Native Americans, the Oto and Missouri, at a place the explorers named Council Bluff, across the river and downstream from present-day Council Bluffs, Iowa. In late October they reached the earth-lodge villages of the Mandan, near the present site of Bismarck, N.D.

Across the river from the Mandan villages, the explorers built Fort Mandan and spent the winter. It was there that they hired Toussaint Charbonneau, a French Canadian interpreter, and his Shoshone wife, Sacagawea, the sister of a Shoshone chief. While at Fort Mandan, Sacagawea gave birth to a baby boy. This did not stop her from participating in the group. She carried the child on her back for the rest of the trip. As a Shoshone interpreter she proved invaluable.

In the spring of 1805 the keelboat was sent back to St. Louis with dispatches for President Jefferson and with natural history specimens. Meanwhile, canoes had been built. On April 7 the party continued up the Missouri. On April 26 it passed the mouth of the Yellowstone River, and on June 13 it reached the Great Falls of the Missouri. Carrying the laden canoes 18 miles (29 kilometers) around the falls caused a month's delay. In mid-July the canoes were launched again above the falls. Later that month the expedition reached Three Forks, where three rivers join to form the Missouri. They named the rivers the Madison, the Jefferson, and the Gallatin, after presidents James Madison and Thomas Jefferson, and Albert Gallatin, who was secretary of treasury under Jefferson.

For some time the explorers had been within sight of the Rocky Mountains.

Crossing them was to be the hardest part of the journey. The expedition decided to follow the Jefferson River, the fork that led westward toward the mountains.

On August 12 Lewis climbed to the top of the Continental Divide, where he hoped to see the headwaters of the Columbia close enough to let them carry their canoes and proceed downstream toward the Pacific. Instead he saw mountains stretching endlessly into the distance. The water route that Jefferson had sent them to find did not exist.

They were now in the country of the Shoshone. Sacagawea eagerly watched for her people, but it was Lewis who found them. The chief, Sacagawea's brother, provided the party with horses and a guide for the difficult crossing of the lofty Bitterroot Range.

It took the Corps of Discovery most of September to cross the mountains. Hungry, sick, and exhausted, they reached a point on the Clearwater River where Nez Percé Indians helped them make dugout canoes. From there they were able to proceed by water. They reached the Columbia River on October 16.

A map by William Clark of the route taken by the Corps of Discovery from the Mississippi River to the Pacific Ocean. Library of Congress Geography and Map Division

On November 7, 1805, after a journey of nearly 18 months, Clark wrote in his journal, "Great joy in camp. We are now in view of the Ocean." They reached the Pacific later that month. They were disappointed to find no ships at the mouth of the Columbia. A few miles from the Pacific shore, south of present-day Astoria, Ore., they built a stockade, Fort Clatsop. There they spent the rainy winter.

On March 23, 1806, the entire party started back. They crossed the mountains in June with Nez Percé horses and guides.

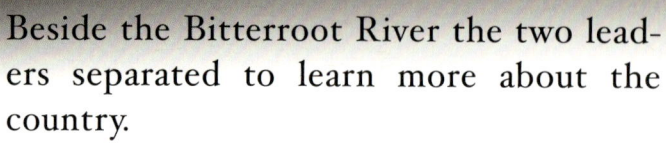

Beside the Bitterroot River the two leaders separated to learn more about the country.

Clark headed for the Yellowstone River and followed it to the Missouri. Lewis, with nine men, struck off toward the northeast to explore a branch of the Missouri that he named the Marias. On this trip he had a skirmish with Native Americans that left two Blackfeet dead, the only such incident of the entire journey. Later, while out hunting, he was accidentally shot by one of his own men. He recovered after the party was reunited and had stopped at the Mandan villages. There they left Sacagawea and her family.

The party reached St. Louis on September 23, 1806. Their arrival caused great rejoicing, for they had been believed dead. They had been gone two years, four months, and nine days and had traveled nearly 8,000 miles (13,000 kilometers).

Later Years

In 1807, following the completion of the expedition, Jefferson appointed Lewis governor of the Louisiana Territory, with headquarters in St. Louis. Lewis's service in his new position was brief. In 1809 he started on a trip to Washington, D.C. On October 11 he was found shot to death at an inn near what is now Hohenwald, Tenn. Some historians believe that he killed himself, while others contend that he was murdered.

CHAPTER 26

WILLIAM CLARK

With Meriwether Lewis, William Clark led the famous Lewis and Clark Expedition of 1804 to 1806 from St. Louis to the mouth of the Columbia River. Lewis was chief in command, but Clark had more frontier experience. More than once he saved the party from disaster.

William Clark was born in Caroline County, Va., on August 1, 1770. He was still a child when an elder brother, George Rogers Clark, won the Old Northwest for the United States. When he was 14 the family moved to Louisville, Ky.

As a youth William helped defend the pioneer settlements against Indians. In 1792 he was commissioned a lieutenant under Gen. Anthony Wayne. Meriwether Lewis served in the same division. Clark was 33 when a letter from Lewis invited him to share the leadership of the expedition. (An overview of the expedition can be found in the Meriwether Clark biography.)

After the party returned to St. Louis, he made his home there. In 1813 Clark became governor of the Missouri Territory. He remarried when his first wife died in 1820. He died on September 1, 1838, in St. Louis.

William Clark, portrait by Charles Willson Peale, 1810; in Independence National Historical Park, Philadelphia. **Courtesy of the Independence National Historical Park Collection, Philadelphia**

CHAPTER 27

ALEXANDER VON HUMBOLDT

Along with Napoleon, Alexander von Humboldt was one of the most famous men of Europe during the first half of the 19th century. He was a German scholar and explorer whose interests encompassed virtually all of the natural and physical sciences. He laid the foundations for modern physical geography, geophysics, and biogeography and helped to popularize science. His interest in Earth's geomagnetic fields led directly to the establishment of permanent observatories in British possessions around the world, one of the first instances of international scientific cooperation. Humboldt's meteorological data contributed to comparative climatology. The Humboldt Current off the west coast of South America (now called the Peru Current) is named after him.

Friedrich Wilhelm Karl Heinrich Alexander von Humboldt was born in Berlin, Germany (then Prussia), on September 14, 1769. He and his brother Wilhelm were educated at home during their early years. (Wilhelm eventually became one of Europe's most noted language scholars

A portrait of Alexander von Humbolt by Mathew Brady.
Science Faction/Getty Images

and educational reformers.) Alexander was at first a poor student and for some years could not decide on a career. Finally botany stirred his interest, then geology and mineralogy. He studied at the University of Göttingen and at the School of Mines in Saxony. In 1792 he obtained a position with the Prussian government's Mining Department. He worked prodigiously to improve mine safety, invented a safety lamp, and started a technical school for young miners. All the while, he was becoming convinced that his goal in life was scientific exploration.

The remainder of Humboldt's life can be divided into three segments: his expedition to South America (1799–1804); his professional life in Paris, where he organized and published the data accumulated on the expedition (1804–27); and his last years, which were spent mostly in Berlin. The Spanish government permitted him to visit Central and South America. This little-known region offered great possibilities for scientific exploration. Accompanied by the French botanist Aimé Bonpland, Humboldt covered more than 6,000 miles (9,650 kilometers) on foot, horseback, or by canoe. After the trip Humboldt went to the United States and was received by President Thomas Jefferson.

Humboldt and Bonpland returned to Europe with an immense amount of information about plants, longitude and latitude, Earth's geomagnetism, and climate. After brief visits to Berlin and a trip to Italy to inspect Mount Vesuvius, he settled in Paris readying the 30 volumes containing the results of the South American expedition.

Humboldt returned to Berlin at the insistence of the king of Prussia. He lectured on physical geography to large audiences and organized international scientific conferences. In 1829 he traveled through Russia into Siberia, as far as the Chinese frontier. The last 25 years were occupied chiefly with writing his *Kosmos*, one of the most ambitious scientific works ever published. In it Humboldt presented his cosmic view of the universe as a whole. He was writing the fifth volume of this work when he died in Berlin on May 6, 1859.

CHAPTER 28

CHARLES DARWIN

The theory of evolution by natural selection that was developed by Charles Darwin revolutionized the study of living things. In his *Origin of Species* (1859) he provided a scientific explanation of how the diverse species of plants and animals have descended over time from common ancestors. The material for this bold theory came from Darwin's voyage around the world in the 1830s.

Charles Robert Darwin was born in Shrewsbury, England, on February 12, 1809. He was an indifferent student who had no interest in the classical languages and ancient history taught in school. Instead, he liked to collect shells, birds' eggs, and coins. He also watched birds and insects and helped his brother make chemical experiments at home.

At the age of 16, Darwin began to study medicine at the University of Edinburgh. There too he found the courses dull, and watching operations made him ill. In 1828 he transferred to Cambridge, intending to become a clergyman. Instead, he devoted most of his time to studying plants and

Portrait of Charles Darwin. Library of Congress Prints and Photographs Division

animals and later to geology. He received his bachelor's degree in 1831.

Then came the event that shaped his life—an appointment as unpaid naturalist on the exploring ship *Beagle*. It left England on December 27, 1831, to chart the southern coasts of South America and sail around the world. The voyage, with many side trips on land, lasted until October 1836. During those five years Darwin examined geologic formations, collected fossils, and studied plants and animals. In the jungles, mountains, and islands he visited, he saw evidence of the many geologic changes that have been occurring over the course of eons—for example, the land gradually rising in some places and falling in others. He also considered the great diversity of living things, even in the depths of the ocean where no humans could appreciate their beauty. He thought about how the fossils he collected suggested that some kinds of mammals had died out. And he returned home filled with questions.

Back home, Darwin settled in London and quietly began work on what would become his great theory of evolution, developed largely in 1837–39. Darwin wrote a short sketch of his theory in 1842 and a longer one in 1844. Instead of publishing the second statement, however, he continued his investigations. Not until 1856 did he begin to write his famous book *On the Origin of Species by Means of Natural Selection*, which appeared in 1859. The theory it presented remains central to the foundations of modern biology.

After completing the *Origin of Species*, Darwin began *The Variation of Animals and Plants Under Domestication*, which showed how rapidly some organisms had evolved under artificial selection, the selective breeding of plants and animals by humans. *The Descent of Man, and Selection in Relation to Sex*, published in 1871, discussed human evolution.

Darwin became very weak in 1881 and could no longer work. He died on April 19, 1882, in Downe, and was buried in Westminster Abbey among England's greatest citizens.

CONCLUSION

Although Native Americans had already lived on the land for thousands of years, Europeans knew nothing of the Americas until Columbus's historic voyage of 1492. The Viking discoveries of five centuries earlier had been largely forgotten. Maps of the time generally showed only a broad strip of land and water reaching from Greenland south to the Mediterranean coasts of Europe and Africa and far eastward to China's Pacific shore.

An increasing curiosity about the world led to the great period of sea exploration known as the Age of Discovery. This curiosity was inspired mainly by commerce. Europeans were looking not for new continents but rather for new sea routes for trade. In fact, Columbus found the New World by mistake. He had been searching for an all-water route from Europe to Asia.

Columbus's chance discovery proved to be one of the great events in world history. Over the course of the next few centuries, European explorers—mostly from Spain, Portugal, France, and England—gradually charted the New World by sea, on rivers, and overland. The settlements they established changed the face of the Americas, irreversibly disrupting Native American culture and installing a European-influenced way of life in its place.

The motives of the New World explorers were many and varied. Some of them continued to look for new trade routes, as Columbus had. Some were seeking wealth and fame. Others wanted to claim new lands for their rulers. A few looked to further their scientific research. And many explorers struck out into the unknown simply for the personal thrill of discovery. Whatever their motives, it is undeniable that their bold efforts fundamentally changed the world in which we live.

GLOSSARY

archaeologist A scientist who studies the material remains (as fossil relics, artifacts, and monuments) of past human life and activities.

armada A fleet of warships.

Aztec A member of a Nahuatl-speaking people that founded the Mexican empire conquered by Cortés in 1519.

ballast To steady something (such as a ship) through the placement of a heavy material.

cannibal One that eats the flesh of its own kind.

cartographer A person who makes maps.

conquistador A leader in the Spanish conquest of America and especially of Mexico and Peru in the 16th century.

Corsica A French island in the Mediterranean, north of Sardinia.

East Indies The islands that extend in a wide belt along both sides of the Equator between the Asian mainland to the north and west and Australia to the south.

galleon A heavy square-rigged sailing ship of the 15th to early 18th centuries used for war or commerce especially by the Spanish.

Hispaniola An island of the West Indies in the Greater Antilles; divided between Haiti and the Dominican Republic.

inlet A bay or recess in the shore of a sea, lake, or river.

isthmus A narrow strip of land connecting two larger land areas.

Jesuit A member of the Roman Catholic Society of Jesus founded by St. Ignatius Loyola in 1534 and devoted to missionary and educational work.

knighthood The rank, dignity, or profession of a knight.

measles An acute contagious disease that is caused by a virus and is marked especially by an eruption of distinct red circular spots.

mercantile Of or relating to merchants or trading.

missionary A person commissioned by a religious organization to propagate its faith or carry on humanitarian work.

monopoly Exclusive ownership or control through legal privilege, command of supply, or concerted action.

mutiny Forcible or passive resistance to lawful authority, such as a concerted revolt (as of a naval crew) against discipline or a superior officer.

New World The Western Hemisphere, specifically the continental landmass of North and South America.

Old World The Eastern Hemisphere exclusive of Australia.

plunder To take goods by force.

scurvy A disease caused by a lack of vitamin C and characterized by spongy gums, loosening of the teeth, and a bleeding into the skin and mucous membranes.

seafaring Making use of the sea for travel or transportation.

smallpox An acute contagious febrile disease of humans that is caused by a poxvirus and is characterized by a skin eruption with pustules, sloughing, and scar formation and is believed to have been eradicated globally by widespread vaccination.

sovereign One possessing or held to possess supreme political power (sovereignty).

strait A comparatively narrow passageway connecting two large bodies of water.

FOR MORE INFORMATION

American Historical Association
400 A Street, S.E.
Washington, DC 20003-3889
(202) 544-2422
Web site: http://www.historians.org
The American Historical Association (AHA) was founded in 1884 and incorporated by Congress in 1889 to serve the broad field of history. It encompasses every historical period and geographical area and serves professional historians in all areas of employment.

Charles Darwin Foundation
Puerto Ayora, Santa Cruz Island
Galapagos, Ecuador
(593) 5 2526-146/147
Web site: http://www.darwinfoundation.org/
The Charles Darwin Foundation for the Galapagos Islands is an international non-profit organization whose mission is the preservation of the Galapagos Islands for scientific research.

Lewis & Clark Trail Heritage Foundation
P.O. Box 3434

Great Falls, MT 59403
(888) 701-3434
Web site: http://www.lewisandclark.org/LCTHF2/HOME.html
Incorporated in 1969 as a nonprofit organization, the Lewis & Clark Trail Heritage Foundation seeks to preserve the Lewis and Clark Trail and history for future generations.

The Mariners' Museum
100 Museum Drive
Newport News, VA 23606
(757) 596-2222
Web site: http://www.ageofex.marinermuseum.org/index.php
Exploration Through the Ages, an online exhibition of the Mariners' Museum, features extensive biographies of world explorers, descriptions of their ships and tools, and an interactive world map and timeline of their voyages.

National Museum of American History
Smithsonian Council for American History
P.O. Box 37012, MRC 619

Washington, DC 20013-7012
(202) 633-1841
Web site: http://americanhistory.si.edu/
The Smithsonian's National Museum of American History dedicates its collections and scholarship to inspiring a broader understanding of the United States and its many peoples.

The Organization of American Historians
112 N. Bryan Ave.
Bloomington, IN 47408-4141
(812) 855-7311
Web site: http://www.oah.org
The Organization of American Historians promotes excellence in the scholarship, teaching, and presentation of American history.

The World History Association
University of Hawaii at Manoa
2530 Dole Street, Sakamaki Hall A203
Honolulu, HI 96822
(808) 956-7688
Web site: http://www.thewha.org/
A community of scholars, teachers, and

students, the World History Association promotes a transnational and cross-cultural approach to the study of human history.

Web Sites

Due to the changing nature of Internet links, Rosen Educational Services has developed an online list of Web sites related to the subject of this book. This site is updated regularly. Please use this link to access the list:

http://www.rosenlinks.com/ioacb/newworbio

BIBLIOGRAPHY

Baker, Daniel B., ed. *Explorers and Discoverers of the World* (Gale, 1993).

Buisseret, David. *The Oxford Companion to World Exploration* (Oxford Univ. Press, 2007).

Cothran, Helen. *Early American Civilization and Exploration* (Greenhaven, 2003).

Cox, Caroline, and Albala, Ken. *Opening Up North America, 1497–1800*, rev. ed. (Chelsea House, 2010).

Edwards, Judith. *Lewis and Clark's Journey of Discovery in American History* (Enslow, 1999).

Faber, Harold. *The Discoverers of America* (Scribner, 1992).

Freedman, Russell. *Who Was First?: Discovering the Americas* (Clarion, 2007).

Ganeri, Anita, and Mills, Andrea. *Atlas of Exploration* (DK, 2008).

George Philip & Son. *Atlas of Exploration*, 2nd ed. (Oxford Univ. Press, 2008).

Konstam, Angus. *Historical Atlas of Exploration: 1492–1600* (Mercury, 2006).

Smith, Tom. *Discovery of the Americas, 1492–1800*, rev. ed. (Chelsea House, 2010).

Stefoff, Rebecca. *The Accidental Explorers: Surprises and Side Trips in the History of Discovery* (Oxford Univ. Press, 2009).

Waldman, Carl, and Wexler, Alan. *Encyclopedia of Exploration* (Facts on File, 2004)

INDEX

A

Almagro, Diego de, 51, 54
Amazon River, 31
America, naming of, 29
Atahuallpa, 53
Aztec Empire, 45, 46, 48

B

Bahamas, 20, 44
Balboa, Vasco Núñez de, 33–35, 39
Brazil, 27, 31, 44

C

Cabot, John, 24–26
Cabral, Pedro Álvares, 27–28
Cartier, Jacques, 63–64
Champlain, Samuel de, 76–79
Clark, William, 104, 106, 109, 110, 112
Colombia, 33, 50
Columbia River, 101, 102, 108, 109, 112
Columbus, Christopher, 16–23, 24, 29, 30, 32
  early life and career, 18–20
  first voyage, 20–22
  later voyages, 22–23
Cook, James, 97–100
Coronado, Francisco Vázquez de, 60–62
Cortés, Hernán, 45–49, 55
Cuba, 21, 22, 32, 45, 48, 55, 57

D

Darwin, Charles, 118–121
de Soto, Hernando, 57–59, 86, 88
Drake, Sir Francis, 65–69

E

Elizabeth I, Queen, 67, 68, 70, 71, 72, 74
Erik the Red, 12
evolution, theory of, 118, 120–121

F

Ferdinand, King, 19, 22, 23
First Nations, 15
Florida, 32, 44, 55, 57, 58
Fountain of Youth, 32
Frontenac, Count de, 84, 88, 92–93, 95

G

Gama, Vasco da, 27, 28

H

Henry IV, King, 76, 78
Henry VII, King, 24, 26
Hispaniola, 21, 22, 23, 33, 45, 50
Hudson, Henry, 80–82
Hudson Bay, 82
Hudson River, 81
Humboldt, Alexander von, 114–117

I

Inca Empire, 50
Indians/Native Americans
  Balboa and, 34
  Cabral and, 27
  Cartier and, 63
  Champlain and, 79
  Columbus and, 16, 20–21, 22
  Coronado and, 60, 61–62
  Cortés and, 46, 48
  de Soto and, 57, 58
  First Nations, 15
  Jolliet and, 88, 89
  La Salle and, 92–93, 95
  Lewis and Clark and, 104, 106–107, 108, 110, 112
  Marquette and, 83, 84, 86, 87
  Narváez and, 56
  origin of term, 21
Isabella, Queen, 19, 22, 23

J

Jamaica, 22, 23, 55
James I, King, 74–75
Jefferson, Thomas, 104, 107, 108, 110–111, 117
John II, King, 19, 22
Jolliet, Louis, 83, 84–86, 88–89, 92

L

La Salle, sieur de (René-Robert Cavelier), 89, 90–96
  attempts to expand New France, 92–95
  early life, 90–92
  final expedition, 96
Leif Eriksson, 12–15
Lewis, Meriwether, 104–111, 112

early life, 104–106
the expedition, 106–110
later years, 110–111
Lewis and Clark
Expedition, 104–110, 112
Louisiana Territory, 90, 95, 106, 111

M

Magellan, Ferdinand, 36–42, 67
Manuel I, King, 27, 28
Marquette, Jacques, 83–87, 88, 89, 92
Mendoza, Antonio de, 60, 61
Mexico, 45–46, 49, 55, 56, 57, 60, 62
Mississippi River, 58, 83–84, 86, 88–89, 90, 92, 93, 95, 96, 102
Missouri River, 106, 107, 110
Montezuma II, 46
Montreal, 64, 90

N

Narváez, Pánfilo de, 55–56
Newfoundland, 15, 26, 44, 63, 97

Northwest Passage, search for, 80, 99

P

Pacific Ocean
Cook and the South Pacific, 97, 98
"discovery" of by Balboa, 33–34, 39, 50
Drake's journey across, 67
Lewis and Clark Expedition and, 108, 109
Magellan's journey across, 36, 39–42, 67
Panama, 33, 50, 57, 67, 78
Peru, 50, 51–54, 57, 67
Pizarro, Francisco, 50–54, 57
Ponce de León, Juan, 32
Puerto Rico, 32

Q

Quebec, 63, 64, 76, 79, 83, 88, 95

R

Raleigh, Sir Walter, 70–75
early life, 70–71
expeditions, 72–74
imprisonment and death, 74–75

S

Sacagawea, 106–107, 108, 110
Spanish Armada, 65, 68–69
St. Lawrence River, 63–64, 78, 89, 92, 93, 97

T

Thompson, David, 101–103
Tonty, Henri de, 93, 95, 96

V

Velásquez, Diego, 45–46, 48, 55
Verrazzano, Giovanni da, 43–44
Vespucci, Amerigo, 29–31
Vikings, 12–15, 24
Vinland, 14, 15

W

Waldseemüller, Martin, 29